FROM AFGHANISTAN TO TEMAZEPAM

The Diary of An SAFC Foot Soldier

Malcolm Robinson

First Published in 2007 by
ALS Publications
1 Hodgsons' Buildings
Stadium Way
Sunderland
SR5 1BT

ISBN 978-0-9550364-5-3

Design & Layout: John Longford & Paul Forrest (*www.alsdesign.co.uk)*
Production Editor: Martyn McFadden
Proof Reading: Sheila Seacroft & Andrew Fury

For more ALS Publications literature and information visit
www.a-love-supreme.com

I would like to dedicate this book with love to my long suffering wife - Angela.

I would also like to thank my parents, sisters, family and friends for their unparalleled support in needy times, it was much appreciated.

Thanks also to Martyn, Sheila, Fury and all at ALS for their hard work and support.

Lest we not forget those who haven't returned from recent conflicts, whose debt we will forever be in.

INTRODUCTION

I'm sitting on the end of the runway at RAF Brize Norton, in Oxfordshire. My chartered Boeing 757 has come to a standstill. I brace myself for the imminent surge of power from the aircraft engines, my hands now gripped, ready for take-off.

Instead of the expected thunderous mechanical roar, the Captain crackles over the in-flight speakers…

"Ladies and Gentlemen, we have just received news that our destination, RAF Akrotiri, has closed, due to a light aircraft accident. Therefore, we regret to inform you, there will be a 24 hour delay to this flight…"

A collective groan greets the unexpected news. Today's flight back from England, to my home base in Cyprus, is operated by a civilian holiday company, meaning the chances of delay were minimal, compared to the Air Force's own evergreen but ageing fleet of aircraft. Yet this twist of fate deals an unforeseen flaw to a seemingly foolproof plan of jetting home today.

The airplane sulks back to the terminal, as everyone on board thinks towards reclaiming their bags and booking a room. However, my thoughts are permanently switched to travelling to London, several cans of lager and Stamford Bridge.

For today, my football team, Sunderland AFC, are playing away at current champions Chelsea and I'm buggered if anyone thinks I'm going to miss this match.

No bags are required and so they are left at the terminal. Everyone else is on their mobiles complaining to loved ones, informing them of the recent news. On the other hand, I am ringing around potential people who are as insane as me, to jump on a train, drink some beer and attempt to watch one of Sunderland's biggest games of the season… without a ticket. It is now 8am so any chance of a native North East chum travelling down from Wearside is slim, and an RAF colleague from down South will have to be persuaded to be my match mate for the day.

One crazy person has been identified and contacted to which the answer was positive. He would be travelling from Swindon and I from Oxford, meaning similar travelling times. We agreed a time and a place (London Paddington) and set about the task in hand.

This is one of the great things about being in the Armed Forces… the camaraderie, the togetherness and more importantly the random banter. It was one of the main reasons I signed on the dotted line back in February 2003. I decided that job opportunities, which were long-term career based, were few back home in the North East. And as reluctant as I was to leave home, I knew I had no alternative, said my prayers and left for life in the Royal Air Force. I had no idea of which direction I was to choose, but the travelling lifestyle of a Movements Controller appealed from the beginning. All I knew was that I would be paid a decent wage to travel the world and experience aspects of life which few get to feel in normal everyday jobs.

As it transpired Movements meant the loading and unloading of aircraft, fully immersed in the world of logistics. This didn't mean a thing to me, still if it meant the option of job security and the benefits that are associated with that, then so be it. I was off to RAF Halton, to engage in a seven week course of basic training, then onto RAF Brize Norton for several months of trade training. From there my first posting was realised at RAF Lyneham, in Wiltshire, where I stumbled through life, not sure if I'd done right in leaving my mother's land. My decision was soon rectified when in late 2004, eighteen months after joining up, I was handed the life changing chance to work at RAF Akrotiri in Cyprus for three years.

I see Wally's face in the distant background, as I step off the train. He wears a smug grin, shaking his head in disbelief that we are here in the nation's capital, after a quick improvised phone call.

"Which pub are we going to?" asks Wally, straight to the point, as any typical Scotsman.

"Wherever mate, I'm easy, as long as it's not too far from the ground," I add.

"What ground is this?" says Wally, now fully perplexed.

"Stamford Bridge… Chelsea… near the posh sorts and all that," I answer.

"What, we're actually going to the match?"

It eventually turns out that our Scottish friend thought we were merely heading towards a pub, to savour the match on large screen, accompanied by a few pints. His face was a picture when I informed him about our match schedule. We decided on a public house near to the ground, thus arriving in time to acquire tickets on the sly. At 3.05pm we had the chance of one ticket, between two for the Sunderland end. Wally nobly offered me the chance to cheer on the lads, while he sat and waited in a local boozer. Then out of nowhere a second ticket appeared, the two of them for various parts of the away section, but at least we were in, we were there.

Through all this I had bumped into my brother-in-law, Al, outside the Londoners' home. To say he was surprised to see me would be the biggest understatement since the phrase 'alright finisher' was used about Kevin Phillips. I informed him not to say anything to his sister about my unlawful presence here and wished him well on his way.

Within around six hours of leaving a dejected air terminal, I was sitting four rows away from Frank Lampard as he whipped in a corner kick for Chelsea. My personal change in fortunes was incomprehensible. And that is why I love the game of football. No other sport relates more closely to life. Both topics generate their own slices of luck-cum-fate, often interlinked with each other, as today's events prove. Had it not been for some unfortunate circumstances back in Cyprus, I would now be about to land on the sun kissed island in the Mediterranean Sea, rushing to the nearest bar, to catch a glimpse of Chelsea versus Sunderland, viewed on a dodgy cable channel. Instead, I'm sat singing my heart out, enjoying the company of a good mate whom I haven't seen in ages, all in the name of football. One can't predict this, just as one couldn't forecast a full time result. That is the beauty of life. That is the beauty of football. More importantly, that is the beauty of living life supporting football.

The game ended in a 2-0 gallant defeat for the lads at the hands of an uncompromising Chelsea side, who would go on to win the title for the second successive season. Little did I know it would be the last Sunderland game I attended, until the lads faced Luton Town, in the offset of a promotion party a season later. For whatever reason that same old foe, fate, decided against me attending another Sunderland game between these times. Something always separated me from seeing my beloved Red and White heroes in the flesh, however whether this was a good thing or bad thing remains to be seen.

Fast-forward under less than a year since my pilgrimage to London and Sunderland AFC are a much changed football club. In that time they have been dumped out of the league on a miserly fifteen points, been overtaken by a consortium of Irish businessmen, Kevin Ball has been and gone as Caretaker Manager, and Niall Quinn has taken the dual role of Chairman/Manager, before appointing the playing legend that is Roy Keane.

The rest, as they will say in the future, is history. In the meantime, the 2006/07 season saw not only a change in my football club but also in my personal life, as my travelling expedition with the RAF led me to the Middle East and the pleasures of Afghanistan in particular. It was on the first day of receiving the news of my impending deployment to the desert that I embarked on recording diary notes, mainly in the first instance to keep a track of courses and important dates I would need to remember. Then as I scribbled away, my feelings fell onto the paper pages, a place in which to absorb into my emotions, which gave a release of sorts. The next stage of events resulted in football making its way into my written thoughts, this then snowballing into the collective diary we see before us now.

For as many on board that delayed flight out of Brize Norton, in September 2005, would have liked to hear the captain to say...

"Ladies and Gentlemen, welcome on board today's flight. We plan to take you to places unknown and emotions untouched. During this voyage, please be certain to look out to the left to see a dull take off, turbulence in between, rounded off by a nice and easy landing, back in the big time..."

"Ladies and Gentlemen, thank you for flying Magic Carpet Airways."

2006/07 was a ride I will never forget. Please remember to fasten your seatbelts.

JULY

Saturday 15th July 2006

Ever since the turn of the year, I have been digging. Through driving rain, hailstone storms and brilliant sunshine, I have never wavered, relentless in my efforts. I have been digging in preparation for times like these – the unwanted times when one's everyday life is turned upside down, wrenched from its shackles, to be left floating along in no direction.

I refer of course to the plight of my beloved football club – Sunderland AFC. And the digging? All worth the struggle to bury my head firmly in the ground, oblivious to events and goings on back home. Sometimes I'm pleased I live over two thousand miles away, adopting an 'out of sight, out of mind' policy. On the flip side, the further I am away from home, the less I can demonstrate, ranting my feelings first hand to the people in charge. I feel less important, as though I might as well stick my thumb up my arse while simultaneously ploughing my head down below.

The club, although now in the hands of Niall Quinn, is still a long way off the pace and standard it requires to mount a promotion challenge back to the top flight. At this point in time I'd be happy with consolidation in the Championship.

No manager, no confidence in players, a feeling of desperation clouding judgement at the SOL.

As it happens it was the start of the pre-season amble today, as Sunderland played down at Forest Green Rovers, in the West Country, against former Rokerite Gary Owers. Do I know the score? No. Do I care at this present moment? No. For the first time in my supporting career, I feel like throwing in the towel, hanging up my match day routine, in favour of origami, or flying kites… well maybe not that far.

My head now firmly in the sand, I pull out a cold beer from the fridge I borrowed earlier and settle down to endless glory days of the Peter Reid era on end of season videos, climaxing into recorded sessions of Premier Passions, where I laugh at Reidy's Scouse man-management ("fucking weak as piss"), and disappear into the memories of life in those heady times, the 185 bus route from the Galleries back to the City centre, Green buses and Sunderland Christmas Illuminations. All long gone, as is the optimism in the atmosphere and dare I say, a lost sense of pride.

Wednesday 19th July 2006

Do you remember when commentators and football pundits use the old cliché "Here's one to pencil into your diary." Well as I have a diary of sorts and a pencil in my hand, I have decided to put the old adage into action.

Here is one for your diaries… Jon Stead scores a goal and in Sunderland colours. Note the game, Rotherham away.

Tuesday 25th July 2006

I found out today that I would be going to Kandahar, Southern Afghanistan in October this year. The boss wanted to speak to me at 8.30am. I initially thought it could have been about anything really. Yet it wasn't until I made my way to her office, did it suddenly dawn on me that it was probably to send me away for four months. And so on this thought I settled myself for the inevitable. The boss had a wry smile on her face, I knew she felt awful passing me my signal and acknowledgement of my deployment, that was just the way she was.

I took the news back to the lads, who insisted on taking the piss, but all in all they were quite respectful, experienced members briefing me on what to do. Even though I knew I was due to be selected to go to war, if felt as though I'd been caught shoplifting, or speeding by the police. That fear of becoming trapped followed by the intense rush of adrenalin afterwards. I had been evading the system since I was ordered to go to Iraq in May 2006, some two months earlier. Only in the advance stages did the orders fall through, leaving me free in the world of Cypriot sunshine - until now. I had been snared like a fox in a trap, with nowhere to go, excuses non-existent. Now was the time to take my deployment instructions on the chin like a man, swallow my pride and admit defeat. You'll never beat the military system… they will always find you.

It was ironic though that on the day my brother-in-law, Andy, flees the hostilities in Afghanistan and is passing through Cyprus on his way home to England, I find out that I'm off in the opposite direction. Our lass, Angela, has been on the phone, but I still haven't told her yet. She will only worry. I could not concentrate myself at work, feeling a sense of unease, anxiety and weird excitement. I will be away over the Christmas period and this will probably upset her the most. I will make sure we have our festive period, either before I go away, or after I return…

…I broke the news to Angie saying I had something important to tell her. She obviously guessed straight away, asking where and when.

"Kandahar in October my love."

This then highlighted the point of Christmas, leaving her upset. She realised we would be missing out on the smaller things in life, for example, I would not get to see our Christmas tree this year. Silly little things, but precious all the same.

Saturday 29th July 2006

What the hell is going on at my football club? Quinny, former legend, now Chairman, now Manager? This type of drama should be reserved for Albert Square and the Queen Vic. There is never a dull moment on Wearside when football enters the equation. I take solace in beer, not knowing whether to focus on my four months away, or the strange goings on at home. In the end I stress over both, leading me to drink vast levels of wine, to stamp out my concern at this early stage for both problematic situations.

Maybe soon we'd see the arrival of Martin O' Neill or Sam Allardyce. I have a nightmare vision of a Terry Butcher/Lawrie McMenemy joint manager package, foiled by the coaching expertise of Mick Buxton, coupled with Howard Wilkinson as Director of Football. Imagine that. I did, producing beads of sweat on my forehead in protest.

AUGUST

Sunday 6th August 2006

The greatest day of the year. Not particularly the date, more so the occasion. I wouldn't tell our lass that, I'd tell her it was the greatest day of the football calendar, but it was better than that.

The opening day of the season, the culmination of two and a half months spent 'dry' without club football, now coming back to life. It's as if it's the day you count out all those saved pennies, before emptying them into the washing machine. When totalling up the amount, you don't realise how much you may have missed those pence, but now they're all back rolled into one big lump sum. All your birthdays come at once, akin to the inaugural day of the football season. The television match day programmes are back previewing the weekend's fixtures, as I simply sit back and absorb the whole build up, oblivious to the outside world. Football's back... oh baby, where have you been?

Forget the horror of Sunderland's Premiership nightmare last season, Niall Quinn and his sublime disco pants are in charge now. I've never seen a Chairman/Manager combo at such a big club as Sunderland. I hope it goes well, not for our sake, but simply for Mr Quinn. He's a legend. Forget that. He's a god up here and this gesture of rescuing our sinking football club is something we can never repay him.

Après – Coventry

A 2-1 defeat. Early days though, but for God's sake what a disaster. We gifted them two late goals, that's the most frustrating thing. Yet we played better football than at any time throughout last season. The squad looks refreshed, let us look ahead.

Still bizarre to see Quinny, Saxton and Robbie Elliott in the dug out. Sacko because it's like seeing a ghost from Christmas past and Elliott, well any ex-Mag is an unusual sight, maybe yet to earn our trust. Lest we forget Lee Clark and Don Hutchison – speaking of whom, was lining up on the other subs' bench. This subject brought the biggest laugh of the day, hearing chants of "one greedy bastard," relating to his supposed quest to leave the SOL, in search of pots of gold. Nice to see our fans still have a sense of humour anyway. I contain my misery with ample amounts of brandy sours and forget the season has started, by basking in the Cyprus sun.

Wednesday 9th August 2006

It's now fifteen days since I found out I was going away for four months to Kandahar. Everything is up in the air at the moment, as obviously my preparations and courses need to be allotted, which inevitably leads to some time back in the UK. That's the only bit of good news, with me hoping to fit in one of Sunderland's games before I depart to the Middle East. The fuckers here are quick enough to send you away to war, but not when it comes to organising the necessary courses. Incredible.

Time to forget Coventry, as Brucey brings Birmingham to the SOL, for Quinny's first home game in charge. I make do with Sky TV's Soccer Special, after enjoying the rare event of a live Sunderland match last Sunday. I like the notion of Wednesday night fixtures, rather than the Tuesday night counterpart. It's a childhood experience thing. When I was growing up, the big teams at the time always played on a Wednesday and it seemed to gain more grandeur. Add to the mixer that my Dad always worked Tuesday nights (the only night he worked) thus meaning I never sampled the unique night match atmosphere for years. So all in all, Tuesdays had strange negative connotations for me.

Anyway, I digress… another game, another miserable night. Clive Clarke, one of Quinny's recent acquisitions from West Ham gave away a penalty on his debut, resulting in the only goal of the night, as Mikael Forssell gobbled away the spot kick. Bollocks.

Saturday 12th August 2006

I dance in and out of sleep, which is probably all well and good, considering what's happening on the box. After taking the lead in the first minute, I awake to see Plymouth leading 2-1 at half time, in Sunderland's third game of the campaign. This was one I in particular needed us to win, for my own personal reasons. Around the corner from my house was my mate Mumf, an ardent Argyle fan. I'd receive abuse all bloody year, until we'd play them again, if we lost. This I could do without, especially as he was on the same shift as me.

I awoke as Stephen Elliott equalized. Mild relief all around. Now we would surely sort out these French tractor boys. Wrong. Twenty minutes later, Plymouth score the winner. Bollocks. No points + three games = lots of abuse, the mathematics were simple. What a shit equation. I look forward to work like a convict sentenced to death.

Apparently, the crowd were having a St Niall's day at today's game. Everyone attending was encouraged to wear green, in honour of Monsieur Discopants' Irish heritage. Pity the luck of the Irish didn't rub off on the team. It's early days though, or so I keep telling the lads at work. This phrase is starting to wear thin.

Saturday 19th August 2006

I stand in shock. Can it get any worse? Southend away and a 3-1 reverse. What the hell is going on at my club? I'm numb, dumbstruck, fucking clueless – like the friggin' team. Quinny, bless him, is not a manager, the bloke is too damn nice. Sounds like the team is too, giving away goals to a side newly promoted. It's a shambles.

The defeat is made worse by watching cockney wide boy, West Ham loving, Ian Beale-esque Tony Cottee, taking great delight in reporting the increasing number of goals for the home side. A good old Essex side, the likes of Tony Gale, Trevor Brooking and Arthur Fowler wank over as their second team. I'm sure he keeps on grinning every time Southend score another.

Can we go any lower? I turn off the TV and disconnect myself away from the cruel, heartless world of football. Surely not another relegation? Not 1986/87 all over again. That would ultimately cripple the club. I dare not think, nor have the energy or will-power to write. I'm sick as a pig. Bring me mid-table obscurity, served cold, any day of the week.

Tuesday 22nd August 2006

A deep dark day indeed. Words cannot express what I'm feeling. I'm obviously on another planet, as I'm all giddy, laughing, even chuckling to myself. I sit down to watch my television set, hoping tonight, in fact expecting tonight will be the night, when Sunderland's fortunes finally turn around. I mean after all we are playing fucking Bury – a team 92nd in the Football league, in the first round of the League Cup. If we lost to them, that would mean at that moment, we would be the worst team in the country, by default. It's like that hypothetical train of thought, in which the first international team to beat the most recent World Cup winners, can be classed as World Champions, albeit by the back door. Joking aside, you could say I was in hysterics by the end of the game, as Bury sink Sunderland by two clear goals to nil. On the outside I may have showed signs of bewilderment, a lack of cohesion disguised in laughter. However, on the inside, I was fucking fuming.

I should have known from the start, when Quinny's new signing, Arnau, from Barcelona was sent off after just four minutes. I merely sat back and watched, resigned to the fact that this would be the lowest we'd been as a football club, for around twenty-one years.

And I watched it all unfold, in what seemed like slow motion. I even think it was Peter Reid commenting on the game in the Sky Sports studio. How strangely ironic?

It was rather peculiar though. At the same time Bury scored (with minutes to go), I felt I was witnessing something incredible, something that Niall wouldn't allow to continue. Sky were loving it, a disaster for Sunderland, a fucking nightmare.

The final whistle blew, and then the real drama unfolded. Niall Quinn was to speak to the awaiting media, with a statement prepared. This didn't sound good, but maybe this was a turning point.

I was now sat bolt upright, paying full attention to Quinn's comments and severe home truths. I felt sorry for him. He looked sick and dejected, as if all his summer aspirations had expired, now out of control. He would step aside, expressing his discontent at our woeful start. Quinn would obviously and thankfully stay at the helm of the club as Chairman, but his managerial days were over. Next big news was that he was lining up a major name for the club, who would be in charge for the next league game. Now I was excited. That's more like it. A major name. This had me scrambling through my brain, raking for names of prime candidates. Curbishley, Pardew, Maldini, Vialli, who else? Allardyce might change his mind, or maybe Martin O'Neill has seen sense.

Forget Bury and the League Cup, this was monumental for Sunderland. This defeat could be our saviour. I just hoped Quinny would stick to his word. I trusted him and so did the rest of Wearside.

Wednesday 23rd August 2006

Quietly enjoying the Charlton – Manchester United game, live on the box, when my Mackem world is turned upside down. It's half time and there I am sipping on a glass of Chilean Merlot as Richard Keys, presenting, turns to the camera…

"Join us after the break, when we'll have news on the vacant Sunderland job."

Well I nearly fucking choked.

Curbishley was in the studio, so maybe, nah. I've got to say that was the longest break, each advert, unwittingly extended by five minutes each. Finally, the match was back.

"We said we had news of the Sunderland job… Roy Keane." Fucking hell. Not what I expected at all. Quality though. I think it took me by surprise. Astonishment in fact. I was put off the scent of Keane, by Quinny's comments, as they'd lined up a world-class manager. Didn't he mean, world-class footballer, or football legend? Anyway it wasn't confirmed, but I hoped it would be. Yeah, he was untried, but he possessed the Old Trafford winning mentality. Surely that would rub off on Wearside. Yeah, bring Keano on. We desperately need him. Immediately I was on the phone to my Dad. He wasn't as keen – no pun intended. Again his untried, lack of experience, the key to my old man's insecurity. Bollocks to that, what a name to bring to the SOL. Come on Keano, sign the contract son.

Thursday 24th August 2006

Needless to say, everyone was pissing their pants, as over a million hits were recorded on the official and fans' websites. Who says Sunderland is not a big club?

Friday 25th August 2006

My head's in a spin. My mind overcome with football and work thoughts. Is Keano coming? Quinny's not happy with the media for letting the story out the bag and I don't blame him. It is also now a month since I was told I was going away on detachment to Afghanistan, yet still no news of courses for deployment training. I have a life to organise too. I know some dates, but they are for a fork-lift course and an aircraft course, but no mention of other dates. I need to book leave, spend time with my wife and family. And of course see a match, especially after all this heightened attention.

I find out that two other lads from my Squadron are to accompany me to the Middle East, one residing in Kandahar with myself, the other one destined for the higher mountainous climes of the capital Kabul. We hear rumours that we will be undertaking deployment training here in Cyprus, which would be a bonus, saving valuable time, which would be spent otherwise travelling back to participate in the same course in the UK.

Still I'm becoming stressed, as nothing is confirmed. I contain my anxiety by producing a list of my biggest fears I may encounter, before and during my four months away.

Kandahar – Biggest Fears
#1- The fear of not returning.

It sounds dramatic I know and although people say the RAF are based inside the perimeter of the airfields out there, well away from the frontline, there remains the fact that one stray bullet or mortar round may come calling and that will be goodnight for you. I suppose this fear leads me onto the next in the list.

#2- Leaving Angela (our lass) alone

Not just for this separation period of four months, but if anything were to happen, I'd be leaving her for good. I don't want her to be by herself. I don't want her to be upset. And I don't want her to struggle to survive. Why should she be the unlucky wife not to have her husband back? She's done nothing wrong, so why should she suffer, when all other partners return home from the conflicts? But then why should anyone suffer?

#3- Being captured

I understand this is another long shot, but I'm a born worrier. I get the genes from me Mam. I suppose I'd rather be like that and cover myself for everything, rather than be slack and under prepared. Though I don't think anyone could be prepared for capture by the enemy.

What would I do in this situation? God knows. I'd like to think I would try and evade my captors, even just to cause as much trouble as possible for them. This is easier said than done, as mock executions and mental torture would rain down, driving me insane, fully demoralised.

#4- My aircraft shot down

This is also an extreme case. However I figure the ratio or probability that the enemy are likely to hit a plane one day is not as slim as people may think. Knowing my luck, this would happen; I'd survive, thus leading back to fear number three.

#5- The unknown

Anybody and everybody must be afraid of something and I'm guessing this phobia would be on the majority of people's lists. How can anyone be afraid of something they don't know or have not experienced? Sounds daft, but at the same time, the mind plays tricks, considering the unknown to be far worse than it is. Am I walking into a killing zone, where mortars are falling down like drops of rain, no time to sleep, terror inflicted into the soul? Or is it peaceful where I'm heading, well away from the action?

Saturday 26th August 2006

Keane will be present at the Bank Holiday Monday match at home to West Brom. Still no confirmation of any deal. Some things will always be the same at Sunderland AFC, they're never rushed.

Sunday 27th August 2006

I felt better penning my worries and fears the other day. This does not detract from my sub conscious constantly mindful of the ever-closer deployment away. I have not aided my cause by asking various members of my Squadron what life is like out there in the desert. And so I've decided to record a synopsis of the varying comments.

Kandahar – The Myth
Funnily enough, I have never been anywhere near Afghanistan, never mind the Helmand or Kandahar provinces of that country. And as keen a traveller of the world and budding Michael Palin explorer as I am, I still wouldn't opt for this Middle Eastern wasteland as a potential favoured destination of mine. It is going to be chez home for four months and so a few of the lads added their inputs on life out there.

One Sergeant did not mind his time there, however this was before the area became extremely hostile. He enjoyed visiting the local bazaar every Saturday. An Afghan flea market, selling an abundance of dodgy merchandise, including the famous Afghan rugs. I could now barter for a slice of my own magic carpet ride, just like the one Niall Quinn had promised us on the start of his regime. He would go shopping with his rifle in tow. I vowed I would not step over the firing line, even if one could buy Red Dwarf box sets for $5.

He added that the weather was variable, as he stayed in the desert in the same timescale as me, only a year earlier. His tour began with scorching temperatures and finished with wind chill factors of −12 degrees. I could handle the cold. Hailing from the North East of England proved this. I gathered that it would be easier to put more layers on when cold, than in boiling heat, when once down to the bare skin, there were no more layers to unravel. The pleasantries of the Sergeant ended here. He moved on to the more disturbing categories of the local wildlife, describing cobras, the renowned camel spider and even wild dogs, surely riddled with rabies. I chose for the information to pass over my head. I would be situated in a tent – not a problem as long as it was already erected.

Others weren't as kind about the place. Kandahar was known as a Category A tour, thus meaning the area was on high alert for attacks. A few lads took the piss commenting that I would be providing "top cover" for the armoured convoys. Bollocks to that, the Army would be better off with Stephen Hawkins protecting their vehicles than myself, such was my poor aim of fire.

Last but not least was the utterance from one of the lads renowned for his lack of words, although always getting straight to the point. When asking where I was heading on detachment and him receiving the answer of 'Kandahar', his immediate but brief response was "What a shithole." I think we'll leave it there, obviously hitting the nail on the head.

Monday 28th August 2006

August Bank Holiday Monday, so why not head down to the local beach. Luckily for us it's a two-mile stretch of sand, surrounded by enclaves of white cliffs, basking in the Mediterranean climate. It's only ten minutes away, so why not make the most of it?

This trip out was then followed up by a glorious barbecue, finished in time for kick off at the SOL, live on Sky. What a day to celebrate the potential signing of

Roy Keane as gaffer. No doubt what all the pre-match hype was concentrated on. The imminent arrival of Keano. And there he was in person, walking through the main marbled entrance at the SOL, where he once walked as Manchester United captain and legend. Quinn was still in charge of team affairs, hoping for a win to sign off on a positive note.

It was a poor crowd in truth, around twenty four thousand, but then it had been five awful defeats in a row. Maybe I'm expecting things to take off too soon. Lest we forget the last two damaging Premiership campaigns. It affected the whole fan base to the core and perhaps requires a long time to rebuild. There were a lot of fans deeply hurt by the embarrassment of those experiences.

Anyway here is to a lively future as Quinny signed off (hopefully for him and the club) with a fine 2-0 win. The players battled like a bastard, something the watching Keane would be proud of himself.

Later that day it was announced Roy Keane was the new Sunderland manager. A day to remember in our history? Well there is a long way to go. Survival will do first, anything else is a bonus, but my crystal bollocks have a positive feeling about this.

Bring it on.

The Birth of The Empire Effect

The first pictures of seeing Roy Keane arrive at the SOL were no less than iconic. As Keano swaggered through the main reception at the ground, he brought with him an air of exuberance and expectation. He expected from us, as we did from him.

The hype and media circus were enormous, with the Sky TV cameras focussing on a football legend. Here was Mr Keane, scrutinising every inch of his new club. The cameras highlighted the meticulous approach of the man, as he absorbed the atmosphere around him, watching from afar in the stands.

It was then that I felt the first taste of optimism I've had in ages. This was all down to the Keano effect, or in my eyes, the Empire Effect. As the cameras zoomed in, the Stadium PA system belted out top indie anthem Empire by Kasabian. With lyrics "We're all wasting away" accompanying the battle cry chorus, it appears the new gaffer has arrived to save our wasting limbs and lead us over the top, hopefully up to the Premiership.

Hence the positive qualities of the Sunderland Empire Effect.

SEPTEMBER

Friday 8th September – The Dilemma

As work continue to bugger me around, I need to focus on travel arrangements home, in order for me to catch a live match. I pencil in a few flights, but to no avail. They are either bank-busting, or inconsiderate dates. I'm sure it would be easier navigating a route back from Timbuktu than Cyprus. We are classed as Europe, which I imagine can only be in name. We must be surely next-door to Australia or Fiji, hence it's a logistical nightmare to fly home.

I must see a live game before I jet off to dustier climes. There is a viable option of a KLM flight, via Amsterdam, which arrives in Ponteland Airport halfway through the Leicester City home game. If I fly back for a week, I could attend the Ipswich away game the following Saturday. It might be my last night on English soil, but I'm sure my family and friends would understand... well maybe.

I've been pissed around numerous times now. Courses given and then courses taken away. What the fuck is going on? Honestly, the main reason people leave the Armed Forces is through the large volume of arsing around and bullshit one has to endure. Anyway, that is the option I'm going for, fingers crossed.

Saturday 9th September

As you can imagine the hype, focus and attention on Sunderland AFC has been immense. International, national, regional, everyone wants a slice of us. I've talked to mates back home and they say they've seen nowt like it. If I could only be there to sample a portion of positivity at long last.

It wasn't just the Keano factor though. The Irishman made six transfer deadline day signings bringing in Dwight Yorke, Liam Miller, Graham Kavanagh, David Connolly, Ross Wallace and re-signed Stanislav Varga. I couldn't believe my eyes. Typically, the internet was down, so I relied on good old ceefax. It displayed a huge list of all the last minute transfer dealings, all undergoing completion, and every second, linked with every league and non-league outfit. Sunderland's name kept on appearing, at every passing glance. We were like rampant rabbits, multiplying all over the shop. It was amazing. I was like a kid in a sweetshop, not knowing where to look next. Add to this the countless notes of speculation and gossip, querying who else might be signing, led me to a light headed state in feeling punch drunk. Never in my lifetime had I seen my football club invest and show their commitment in signing players so openly. But not just the usual run of the mill shite, these were decent players.

I just couldn't comprehend, nor absolve this new revolution. Where once we made do, putting up with second best, now we had winners in charge and determined players eager to succeed. I may be getting carried away at this very early stage, but sod it, we all deserve a little positivity in our lives.

The fans back home agree, as we take over four thousand to Pride Park, Derby, in Roy Keane's maiden match. Watching on TV, I find that Sky seem more interested in Keano's reactions and whether he'll explode into a combustion of rage and temper, at the slightest hint of a bad refereeing decision. To be honest, I too was intrigued by this factor and when Derby scored on half time, I would have loved to be a fly on the wall in the away dressing room. This would be Keane's first major test.

And of course, he passed it. Sunderland gradually showed signs of prowess in front of goal. Then eruption at Pride Park, as four thousand travelling Mackems went mental, along with Keane and the Sky reporter. I joined in the celebrations, as Chris Brown scrambled in the leveller.

A minute later it was two and I was dancing in the living room. My two cats were going wild, as my bellows must have scared the shit out of them. I can only imagine the delirious scenes at Derby. Ross Wallace marked his debut by scoring and celebrating in with the fans – pure quality. That's what we want, a display of passion, smitten with character and pride… sheer fighting, gutsy pride. And with that our first away win, our first back to back wins, not forgetting Keane's first win in a baptism of fire.

Wednesday 13th September 2006

No time to lose, keep those wheels turning, keep the fires burning. Hold those thoughts, as we ply our trade at Leeds away, who are themselves spluttering with intent at present. Their fans are envious. They hate our gaffer but Mr. Keane would want it no other way. Second game in charge, Leeds away, meaning another consecutive four thousand plus away following. Wearside has come alive, making up time after our lie in to the new Championship season.

I admit I was flicking through various sports channels, not wanting to concentrate too hard, possibly nerves, perhaps just wanting my team to carry on this trend, but not to expect too much just yet.

It was Reidy again in charge of the reporting on Sky, commenting that Sunderland were all over Leeds, like crabs on overtime in a brothel. I always fear the worst when pundits say this. Usually, sod's law dictates that the opposition will inevitably go up the other end and score. Not this time. Another new signing Liam Miller scored a sensational opener and we were off. Another check at half time and it's now 2-0. This time fellow new boy Graham Kavanagh took his chance to record his version of goal of the season. Jesus, we were going wild at Elland Road. These fuckers were one game shy of the Premiership last season under Kevin Blackwell and look at us pissing all over their front windows. The natives will be restless. They won't take kindly to their old enemy Sunderland running the show.

I expected a comeback from Leeds, but nothing transpired. I glanced again, literally minutes after half time and 3-0 flashed up on the box. We were awesome, as Stephen Elliott grabbed a third. I don't know what's going on, but Keane must have the magic touch. I bet Harry Potter has been handed his P45, thanks for everything, but Keano's the real wizard now son. 3-0 up at Leeds, we've never had it so good there.

I was gonna stick on me pads and find me bat, to indulge in this potential cricket score. This didn't materialise, though a 3-0 away win can't be scoffed at. I'd been at Elland Road the last time we beat United, in Mick McCarthy's Championship success. It was great then and that was only 1-0. Imagine 3-0; imagine the scenes, the delirium.

Friday 15th September 2006

I've settled for the Amsterdam diverting flight back tomorrow, in order to visit my motherland. News from back home is somewhat disturbing. My parents have informed me that one of my sisters is travelling to the North East to see me next weekend and so any ideas about going to the Ipswich match better be cancelled" I don't fucking believe it. I fucking told everyone I had plans for the away game in Suffolk, but obviously to no avail. They surely must have thought I wasn't serious. I definitely was though. Bastards, as much as I want, need, to go, I can't not see my family. For one I'm too soft and for seconds, I'd never hear the end of the matter.

Ipswich was cancelled, Leicester was too late, and I'd have to rely on a training ground session to capture a moment watching the lads in action.

Bollocks to life and the Armed Forces. If I had kept my original course dates, I would have attended numerous games.

Saturday 16th September 2006

I'm back in Blighty, having flown on Cyprus Airways (on behalf of KLM) via Amsterdam, then from the Dutch capital to Tyne and Wear's joint tax paying aerodrome. It feels like I've travelled from Zanzibar, never mind Cyprus. It would be easier getting back. In fact I'm gonna look on the internet to see if it is easier, just to prove a point. Anyway, I'm here now. It's fucking fantastic to be back in the North East. Not much changes, but then do I want it to? That would spoil the beauty of returning home. We moan on that everything stays the same, then loved ones comment, you haven't missed much. Well it's just everyday life isn't it? I'd be gutted if an earthquake disintegrated the region and we were back visiting survivors. Nah, keep it the same, keep it real. What's wrong with visiting the city centre, popping into Joplings to keep our lass sweet, placing on a bet, chomping away on a Greggs' cheese and onion pastie, or munching through a savoury dip, topped with pease pudding, or a fish lot from Clem's?

Going for a stroll down the sea front at Seaburn, walking along to Roker, down the Cat and Dog steps, through the park, along Sea Road, order a short back and sides from Fellaz, then off to the Mill View Social Club for a pint of Stones and put the world to rights. Nothing wrong with that. Add shopping at the Metro Centre (although I do get a headache after a while), swimming at the Crowtree, a night down Green Lane, waking up at your mate's in Penshaw, passing the Monument on the journey back, meeting the missus in town for an Italian lunch at Luciano's, to soften her up after getting pissed and staying out. A touch of class.

Everyone moans on because everything is taken for granted. I whinge on in Cyprus and look at me, the Mediterranean Sea around the corner, Troodos Mountains in the distance and my homemade bar – The Red and White Tractor. All taken as everyday life, only appreciated when one is deprived of it, does one really value their attraction.

Speaking of attractions, the main one was the match, something I was missing out on. I did secretly hope for someone from the club to be waiting at the Airport, to whisk me to the game, that day versus Leicester. After writing a cheeky letter to Niall Quinn, stating how I would like the game that day to be delayed twenty-four hours, or to an evening kick off, I half-heartedly hoped for some kind of gesture from the club.

Who am I kidding? I don't mind though. It was a Chris Makin-type shot in the dark, a bit of banter. As it was I consoled myself with a few pints in an Irish bar, quirkily tucked away in a sun terrace within the confines of Amsterdam Schiphol Airport. It was a cool little place, situated oddly enough in between terminal buildings. I had me Guinness to act as luck for the day's forthcoming fixture with the Foxes.

I was met by my Dad off the plane, who swiftly informed me that City had taken the lead just after half time. Cheers, Dad, nice to see you too. I had a hissy fit and refused to listen to the radio, deciding on conversation instead, whilst eyeing up the North East scenery.

We arrived home just in time for Sunderland's equalizer. Me Mam goes… "Hi son, good journey, Hussein's just scored."
"Who?" I ask, ah Hysen, I acknowledge – quality. I'd travelled over two thousand miles and here I was ten minutes from the SOL, on a Saturday afternoon watching the old exiles' favourite Soccer Saturday. The TV programme was my old pal from back in Cyprus, with whom I'd share Saturday afternoons. Frustrating is not the word, more like sick, devastated, or grief-stricken. But it was brilliant to see everyone, so I suppose I can't grumble.

I was handed a pile of Football Echos, programmes and fanzines to sift through, a mug of tea, home made corned beef pie, as we watched the results flow in. It ended 1-1 down the road, still keeping Keano's unbeaten run intact. I was now on full alert to see the crowd walk past our mum's house, something I'd do as a child, when I couldn't get to a game. It was still a part of the match day experience to see the locals trundle back, no doubt faces a lot happier than last season, with an added spring in everyone's step. Wait half an hour, and then I'd be over the paper shop to collect that day's Footy Echo, as if I'd been to the match. Chitchat in the shop, then back home, trying in vain to pass The Grange public house without peering in, opting for a pint. With my head down, I walked with steadfast even tread, scurrying back home to analyse results and league tables. There, in front of me, another aspect of football culture we all take with a pinch of salt – The Football Echo. It's fair to say that not many regions can boast an evening sports supplement at the weekend anymore. This can hold true for the Mags and the Chronicle's Pink publication. A dying breed, thanks to the modern game kick off times and saturation of the nation's sport. I wonder how much Sunderland's yo-yo culture has inadvertently saved our own Footy Echo from going under? I would like to think it would be bought regardless if Sunderland played Friday night, Saturday afternoon or Sunday morning, to keep our traditions alive.

Anyway, I digress…

Canny crowd today for Keane's first home game. 35,104, make that 35,105, if I'd been present. Still, I've arranged for me and me Dad to visit the Academy for a glimpse of a training session. That'll have to be the next best thing, considering the circumstances.

Thursday 21st September 2006

I have just returned from the Academy of Light. It was my first visit and my first impressions were of colossal top class facilities, something that must have turned Roy Keane's head. There was a maze of fucking alleyways from the public car park that would have been vastly exploited by hooligans, if it had been situated outside some 1980s terraced ground. At one point we were off to see Kevin Ball's youth team, as we took a wrong turn.

Eventually, we found a fifty, sixty strong crowd, to be informed that the first team squad were half an hour delayed and would be appearing shortly.

Bobby Saxton appeared first, the one time assistant coach, now surely a passing advisor to Roy, but nothing more. Still he deserves a big pat on the back, stepping in the breach, when a void needed filling. We were there for three and a half hours in total, which pissed our lass off no end. I informed her that I hadn't come all this way to see bugger all. She politely replied that I was a mental case, but she still loved me. At least I wasn't the only head case, as my dad and brother-in-law, Al, watched the new regime put the lads through their paces. All the players were in high spirits, as we laughed at games of piggy in the middle. In one particular instance, Keano was the piggy, still going through the men to retrieve the ball back. Does this bloke have to win at everything? Hopefully, he can instil this into the players, who seem to be enjoying the training.

I arrived at the Academy, armed to the maximum, in order to collect autographs. I thought I might as well, seen as I'm here. What really made me sad according to my missus was carrying around my Panini World Cup '06 sticker album (full of course) to be signed by the newly acquired Trinidad and Tobago international – Dwight Yorke. What she didn't know was that I'd planned to get the whole album signed by the time the next World Cup starts. Also present were the recent home programmes against Birmingham and Plymouth, ready and waiting for signatures. Obviously, Roy Keane was the prime target, Yorke second and anyone else after that. I'd also brought along a camera for a photo with the legend Keane too.

We took in my last match before I departed for the desert of Afghan, albeit a practice game between the first and reserve team squads. Still a chance to see all the new signings on show, Kavanagh looked sharp, as did Miller, both the Millers in fact. The young Spaniard – Arnau - had a few deft touches in his locker. Things look promising. The one memory I'll take away with me though, was the sight of our new gaffer, sat on one of the grassy mounds that surround the training ground. He was perched at the top, arms folded, quietly sat in methodical reflection, looking on at his new bunch of players. It screamed of classical connotations of Brian Clough, and if Roy can pull off any of the great man's techniques, then Sunderland are in for a treat.

I was now becoming nervous at the fact I had to ask Keano for a photo. The training ended with the manager chatting to his troops, every one of them focussed on his words of wisdom. Then they all began to trek back to the Academy buildings. My heart was pounding now, like a daft kid, wanting to see his heroes. I suppose I've never grown up when it comes to football. Some would argue, I've never grown up.

Keane was the first one off the pitch, I mumbled "any chance of a photo?" as the great man snatched my two programmes out of my hand, scribbling away – still walking at marching pace. There's me scrambling after him, like some kind of lap dog. He finished his signature and promptly ploughed into the awaiting army of fans. And that was that. My photo opportunity had vanished… still I had his autograph. Al stood laughing at me, adding I was like a squirrel on heat, running after the bastard, wanting me programmes back.

An assortment of players barged past next, as we took incoming first teamers from every angle of attack. I took the prized assets of Kenny Cunningham, Liam Lawrence, Graham Kavanagh and the ex-Barcelona B skipper, Arnau. Still Dwight Yorke lingered around with one of the backroom staff. Eventually, he came over, complete with that famous smile on his face. He was happy to converse with anyone and everyone and more to the point was pleased to have his photo taken with yours truly, as well as signing his own World Cup sticker, like a legend he is. Quality, fucking dancer. All this made my year, a good send off indeed.

The day then rounded off with a picture with a Wearside great. Before my time, but remembered with pride. A picture of me and the recently unveiled Bob Stokoe statue – a fitting end to any Mackem's day. Not to mention, the pile of match day programmes which I had reserved at the Sunderland Supporters shop, opposite the ground, but we'll keep that one quiet from our lass. I sneak the ever-growing collection of away programmes through me mother's front door. Quality day indeed.

Saturday 23rd September 2006

The last day of my UK break and the day of the game in which I was hoping to attend. Only Ipswich away isn't a quick sortie down the road, a la Barnsley or Leeds. To Suffolk and back, say bye to all the family, before I go to war, well it wouldn't work. I'd get shunned by me parents, besides, sometimes football has to take a back seat – not very often mind – but on this occasion, well family is important.

As it turns out, a shite day at the office for the lads. We crumble to a 3-1 defeat, not even managing to score our goal. Thank fuck I never took the match option, deciding to enjoy the whole day with relatives.

Bollocks to it, a sour end and Keano's first defeat. That ends the notion of an unbeaten run until the end of the season, as some quarters in the North East predicted. A tad carried away I presume?

I find that having leave back home can be something of a nightmare. It's not the fact I hate going home, I love the place. That is why I seem to count down the days I have left, making the time go even faster. I found that this time I had missed so much of what I had planned to do, hoping I would have the chance to undertake these pleasures next time I visit, if there was a next time.

My last night at home was panicked and emotional. There is a whole combination of things that I miss about North East life, one being the weather. And it's not until one lives away in the barrage of humidifying heat, that you appreciate the milder climate of home. There is one ingredient on the Wearside weather menu, that stands out from the rest is fog. A strange choice, but fog is something to behold and stand in awe of.

My parents live ten minutes away from the North Sea and the surreal reality of the mist and fog floating around the streets is unreal. It is to be best enjoyed at night. I recall supping a few cheeky pints of Stones and with the bitter running around my body; the calling of the chippy over the road is immediate. Armed with a portion of chilli and chips, doused in lashings of malt vinegar, one would proceed with the ten-minute walk home. Everyone else had gone to bed, bar a few roving taxis. The night air belonged to me, as the mist descended, now fully engulfing my body.

And then out from nowhere, the night atmosphere would be bombarded with a throbbing base of noise, which would both pierce your eardrums, as well as the cloudy night sky. A bellow of a foghorn, first with a muted aperitif, then followed by the main event, as the siren serenaded the stranded vicinity, this time in stereo monotones, then disappearing leaving the night silent once more. The sea air swarms around you, like baying sharks, circling their prey.

It was a joy then on my last night at home, stepping outside for a gentle stroll in the back garden, relaxing in a break away from the concerted hustle and bustle of a family dinner, when the night air revealed an ambient tune of foghorns and the freshness of the murky sea air. I stood there on luscious turf, looking like a crazed man, merely breathing in the smell of the nearby sea, the smell of home, transfixed by the lonely tune of the foghorn. This made me sad. It was like nature saying goodbye, or was it my paranoia setting in? Was this the last time I would hear this local ensemble, unique to me?

With a tear in my eye, I ventured inside, wishing that this night would never end and I could stay in my tranquil bliss, surrounded by my wife and family, for a series of endless days. I take it as a simple good luck send off, not a final goodbye. I hope to be back in the mist of the North East, demolishing my chips, mixed with vinegar overtures, enclosed by my fog and its horns come the New Year.

Sunday 24th September 2006

I leave the North East for the last time, before I head towards the unknown hostilities that lie ahead in Afghanistan.

My heart is filled with woe, as all my goodbyes are said. I've counted down the final few days, as if I were waiting for a time bomb to explode. I only hope it won't be the final time I see my homeland. Probably not, but one can't help having these negative thoughts running around my head. Not everyone comes back from a war zone, but I made a vow that I would return – ready of course to take in a match, watching my red and white lads. I fucking love Sunderland.

We arrived at the airport before a sensible hour was reached. In these circumstances, my Dad would drop us off by himself, not this time as my Mam accompanied us too, which was nice. We checked in and slowly made our way upstairs to the departure lounge. My Mam gave me the tightest squeeze I'd ever had off her. As she hugged me, she whispered how much she loved me and how I was to take care. I could have stayed there forever. She was upset. I tried to get the words out about how much I loved her, but they simply wouldn't come. There was no sound coming out my mouth.

It was then my Dad's turn, who told me the same. And still no words would arrive. I simply nodded. I think he knew if I spoke, I would blabber my conversation. That was it, a final wave goodbye, time to move on, I only hoped that I would see them again.

It is strange what life throws at you. Do people in the Armed Forces ever become fed up of saying goodbye? It's all I ever seem to do these days. Sometimes I get tired of it all. Sometimes I think why don't I have a job, where I live locally and do normal routine stuff. It is then I think how lucky I am to be in the Armed Forces. We are looked upon with pride by the nation, and rightly so. Maybe one day I'll settle down.

Anyhow, the clinky clink of the drinks trolley helps quell my despondency. I feel light-headed on our sojourn around Amsterdam on the return trip, finally catching the last leg of the trip back to Larnaca, complete with my bag of Sunderland goodies, ready to show the lads, akin to the playground once more.

My only hope is that my Black Cats are on the verge of something big on my return. But for now I'd settle for stability, ready to push on next season.

Saturday 30th September 2006

We bounce back from the defeat at Portman Road, with a businesslike 1-0 home win over Sheffield Wednesday, thanks to Grant Leadbitter. Another huge crowd of 36,784 also boosted no doubt by Wednesday's massed ranks of travelling fans. I resorted to viewing Soccer Saturday, once more this time 2,000 miles away. Yet the victory is just as sweet. Whether I'm around the corner from the SOL, or basking in the Cyprus sun, a win is a win, as we climb further away from the relegation zone.

I try to enjoy the victory, but my impending date with deployment away is playing on my mind. This seems to be the worst possible time, like a sitting duck, waiting for the final curtain and my exit to the sand dunes of the desert.

Part of me wants to suspend time, allowing me never to visit Afghanistan, whilst the other part wants to fast forward and go there today, thus getting the punishment over with, then settling back into normal life.

OCTOBER

Saturday 7th October 2006

This weekend saw my usual match day routine disrupted thanks to international games taking place. This was, though, a huge slice of saving grace for me. I always check to see who Cyprus are playing, taking advantage of my geographical location. I'd already taken in a Cyprus v. Wales friendly the other year, and also the unusual round robin free for all that is the Cyprus International Football tournament. Where else would one have the chance to watch footballing greats like Armenia, Greece, Iceland and fucking Belarus battle it out on lumpy pitches? To be fair the ticket was only a fiver. On this occasion Cyprus by a twist of fate were entertaining the Republic of Ireland, in the capital – Nicosia.

For my send off, my good mate Spit decided to drive me all the way there in style, in his convertible motor. Not a bad way to travel to the match eh? I was to be Sunderland's ambassador to the Irish, spreading the good word of Niall and Roy's red and white revolution. For this reason I donned the sacred cloth of Wearside colours, beach shorts, grey Lacoste flip flops and pair of Police sunglasses, in order to pull off the Danny Dyer, rogue, ex-con, fun-loving Mackem gangster effect. As rural Cyprus flashed by, cans of crisp Carlsberg were necked, adding a flavour of Britain to the festivities.

We had no tickets, but that was the beauty of it all. Where else could you turn up at a significant international qualifier on the day of the game and click through the turnstiles, without question? Well that was the plan anyway. I had visions of sold out signs greeting our arrival, as the Irish juggernaut rolled into town.

The GSP stadium holds around 23,000 - more than enough to accommodate the home team's pulling power, with football taking a back seat over here, well at least the Cypriot side. They'd rather watch fucking Greece than sit through the third division standard of football fare on offer. Nevertheless, this arena is still a tidy ground, boasting a sail-like main stand that arches over the remaining three quarters of uncovered seating, not too dissimilar to Lord's, The Oval or other cricket grounds. Canny enough for our day out. My early fears were allayed, as we turned up early to buy our tickets, for the Irish end of course. We had sat in the Cypriot end on earlier visits, but that was mainly to piss the Welsh lads off. Besides, I was now an honorary Celt, eager to join in the fun and madness that revolves around the Irish followers. My football club was now more than half Irish; fuck England and the miseries of Steve McClaren's tactics. Fucking Lampard, Rio and Jamie Redknapp's old boy's network, in which the England side can do no wrong. Watching prim donna wankers soil the three lions badge and Ashley Cole pretending to be a footballer.

Pass me the Irish charm and the happy go lucky attitude, the unpredictability of the team and most of all, the laid back unity of the travelling hoards. We were greeted with chants of "Roy Keane's Red and White army", mixed with cries of "Niall Quinn's disco pants", as Spit and I networked with the followers from the Emerald Isle. The locals weren't so friendly with regards to ticket prices. The cheeky twats decided to charge Cypriot fans a tenner and us – the Irish - thirty quid a pop. It's a fucking disgrace, but not only a phenomenon of these shores. It brought back numerous memories of clubs back home overpricing travelling Sunderland supporters, in a bid to cash in on our loyal reputation. Bollocks to it, Spit wanted to enjoy the atmosphere and spur on the boys in green. Thirty notes it was, with asking the ticket office for directions to my seat, seen as they'd just taken my fucking eyes out, the robbing bastards.

It was onto the continental bar fixed to the side of the ground, as we supped away with green, gold and white floating around us. On the journey around to our stand, we swapped banter, whilst pissing ourselves at two Cypriot TV reporters trying to broadcast, with drunken Ireland fans in the background. At one point, one of the Republic lads took charge of the microphone, producing his own version of events to puzzled local onlookers. We were in hysterics, as I snapped it all on camera for prosperity.

It was also my chance to see Sunderland players in the flesh for the first time this season, however with Kavanagh and Elliott withdrawing from the squad, my last chance was Liam Miller. Without any official news of the starting line up and the fact the Irish players all looked alike, apart from John O'Shea and Paddy Kenny, I had difficulties in completing my initial task.

Anyhow, the match was enjoyed, even though Cyprus took the lead. We all felt that Ireland would equalise, to which they did, but what followed was unreal. The Republic defence were awful and Cyprus looked like scoring on every attack. This resulted in a shock 5-2 victory for the home side, as chants of "Stan Out" rattled around the ground, referring of course to manager Steve Staunton. It was Cyprus' record international home win, I suppose something to tell the grandchildren. Still the Irish fans held firm, chanting their side to the finish line, still exchanging banter and no sign of bother.

Lo and behold another member of the Mackem allegiance was spotted, as we swapped stories and posed for a quick photo, both agreeing to the newfound optimism back in the North East under Roy Keane. We sneaked out with the Irish contingent of buses, as home traffic came to a standstill. It was like a normal away day, watching Sunderland. And what better way to round the day off, than to pick up a Ruby Murray, on our way back through the city of nearby Limassol, en route home. Meanwhile, back in the sitting room world of Sky Sports, England spunked their way to a goalless draw at home to Macedonia, thus vindicating our decision to go Irish for the day. More of these capers and I'll be buying a ticket for the new Lansdowne Road, rather than the new Wembley... well at least until McClaren and most of the short sighted FA committee fuck off.

Sunday 8th October 2006

I wake up in a drunken slumber to discover my camera's memory card, holding all the great memories of the Irish jig that was yesterday's drama, had packed in, deciding to delete the entire collection of photos. Bollocks.

Tuesday 10th October 2006

Today was the first day of my combat training course in preparation for the possible terrorist threat ahead. My two mates have joined me, adding to the banter of the otherwise nervy occasion. Lectures after lectures were the order of the day, covering a wide range of subjects from health issues, cultural aspects of Afghanistan, identifying various types of snake and dealing with gunshot wounds and ballistics.

The intelligence brief was the most interesting of the day, shedding light on recent activity out there, whilst also outlining the long-term history of the hostilities in the region. We also received the news we would be awarded two medals for serving in the desert. For some medals mean nothing. People expressing that they were simply doing their job. Perhaps a medal of honour à la VC or the Queen's Gallantry medal were something worthy of merit, as winners performed tasks out of the ordinary, often resulting in the saving of lives. Other people share a different outlook, even going so far as volunteering for different war regions, to gain their own personal collection of silverware, otherwise known as military tourism.

Personally, I would not go as far as offering my services towards varying conflicts around the globe, however I regard the receiving of a medal as a token gesture for one's efforts in what I believe will be the hardest four months of my life. It is a little piece of personal history, a small keepsake.

Wednesday 11th October 2006

I received all of my combat kit, required for the task in hand in the coming months. I feel up for the fight now. It's like a junior football team receiving their first professional kit. I now look and feel the part. I say if you are well equipped and feel wanted/protected, then as a person, you are likely to perform to a higher degree.

Still, I'm brought down to earth with information on what to do if captured.

Thursday 12th October 2006

Today was what I would consider the first phase of proper training. We were taught anti-ambush drills, amongst other fighting skills. It was then off outside to practise what we were taught, luckily only receiving blank ammunition, rather than the real world of full metal jackets.

Now fully briefed, we were split into Charlie and Delta teams (minus Chuck Norris in the latter) and the ambush was underway.

On the command of "contact" (substituting the real sound of enemy gunfire) we exited our vehicle, spraying the supposed target with blanks, the crackle of rounds spurring on the adrenalin now fully flowing around the system. Smoke grenades were lobbed, as we peeled off into defensive formation. This shit was pulsating; though I remember thinking I'd rather not do it for real.

The exercise was over in an instant, with streams of sweat pouring from every part of my body. This was Cyprus in October; hence it's relatively warm. I began to imagine participating in the same kind of drills in the unforgiving inferno of the Afghan summer. Considering we were tradesmen first, soldiers second, our instructor was hugely impressed with our efforts.

We pissed ourselves laughing afterwards about the numerous minor cock ups of abuse of safety catches and magazine changes, as well as the fact that one of the lads tried to fire as few shots as possible, in a vain attempt to maintain a clean rifle. This notion became flawed when our instructor ordered everyone to switch our weapons to automatic (a machinegunesque mode) and fire off any remaining rounds. This soon had us in fits again, until his empty discarded round jackets showered me in a deluge of piping hot golden metal.

I was pumped up for hours afterwards. I bet our lass thought her husband had transformed into MacGyver walking through the door that evening.

Saturday 14th October 2006

We've apparently got another huge following today at Deepdale, Preston North End. Around 6,000, which considering the club has just been relegated with the full embarrassment of fifteen measly points is unbelievable. It's the Keane factor in stereo mode. North End have even turfed all of their season ticket holders into adjacent stands, to accommodate the awesome away following.

It's a fucking shame then, that Preston wallop us 4-1, with them being four up at half time. Every time Sunderland has the chance to perform and reward the fans, they fluff their lines.

Clearly, there is still a load of problems lurking around the club and team in particular and it would be foolish to suggest otherwise. Roy hasn't got a magic wand, although his evil stare has been known to work wonders. We'll all have to be patient – something I'm afraid doesn't come easily to us Sunderland fans.

Stan Varga netted a consolation goal, his first on his return to Wearside and that's all for positivity today. The quicker we forget that the better.

Monday 16th October 2006

I go about chasing up my flight details for my journey into the unknown world of Afghanistan. Being in the Movements trade enables perks and privileges, mainly in the shape of seats on flights, in prime locations on the aircraft. In this instance, I have already spotted a potential flight into the desert, firstly stopping off overnight in Qatar, then onto Kandahar airfield, the whole experience taken in onboard a Hercules cargo plane. This would be a more direct flight than the usual hassle of flying back to the UK, then travelling another seven hours to my destination. It also allowed me to arrive four days earlier, killing two birds with one stone, meaning everyone was happy. Firstly the lad I was replacing would be able to fly home quicker and I'd rid myself of this long dreaded wait, hanging over me.

It was looking good, that I would have a seat booked on this Hercules flight. Knowing the realms of Sod's law as I do, I thought it would be well worth a check on my reserved flight details. After all, the old adage goes, "prior preparation prevents piss poor performance." I was handed my details in the Admin department, with the UK piss about on paper in its full glory. I was to fly from Cyprus to Brize Norton, wait a few hours and double back on myself, arriving in the Afghan capital, Kabul. And that is where the itinerary of travel arrangements ended. I queried the lack of details, for my onward journey down south to Kandahar, to receive the answer that I will probably finish off this gruelling trip by road. I laughed in his face, telling the lad I'd make my own travel plan. Go by road? Are you mad? I'd be a sitting duck, travelling all that way, seeing those anti-ambush skills as a necessity to survive.

I popped into work to confirm my initial flight details and so the Hercules it was. I'd never flown in one before, adding to the whole unknown original fear element surrounding the saga.

Tuesday 17th October 2006

My last Sunderland game to watch in comfort, as Afghanistan awaits. It's Stoke City away, with the Potters fielding on loan Rory Delap from Sunderland. A tad strange, surely Keano would have insisted on a clause in his contract whereby Delap would not be eligible to play against his main employers.

In the end it proved to be an awful night for the lad, breaking his leg in a challenge with Robbie Elliott. Football is a cruel, twisted game. What are the chances of that happening against your own club? I still think Delap can do a job for us, to quote a classic Peter Reid saying, and so I feel upset to hear the news. Things don't get any better performance wise, as we lose 2-1, after Dwight Yorke scored his first goal for us. Early days though. Not a good send off for me, compounding my fear and loathing, at my impending four months of shite.

I'm afraid to say that football is on a back burner at present, as I concentrate on ensuring all my kit is in order, even though I've only just received most of it. Talk about lastminute.com. I feel on edge constantly, snapping at the slightest of strains everyday life throws my way. It's as though I'm off to prison for four months. It really is a weird feeling, unsettling, and waiting to say my long good-bye to my wife, not knowing if I will see her again. What the fuck did I sign up for? Certainly not some bollocks of a war that no one gives a shit about back home. But I take the paycheck every month, so I will swallow my bitterness and carry on with the job in hand.

Wednesday 17th October 2006

There was a classic episode of a Mediterranean thunderstorm tonight. It was undoubtedly brilliant, as fork lightning flashed voltage across the night sky. Our lass and I decided to visit a new restaurant, virtually holding our own personal dining in night, due to the lack of other guests, which was perfect for one of our few remaining evenings together.

The topic of Afghanistan was never too far away, waiting on the fringes of con-versation, ready to intervene with its ugly head, to remind us why we were out.

This week has been the longest week ever, most like waiting for one's main stage role in a public hanging. I know it is going to happen, but I can't do anything to stop it. I do receive a stay of execution; my flight is already delayed 24 hours. I don't know whether this is good or bad news. The thunderstorm takes my mind off any worries, the power now cut off, relying on candlelight to continue the evening's charm.

Saturday 21st October 2006

I imagine what would be happening now if I was still in Sunderland, hanging around with my mates, enjoying life living at my parents' house, without a care in the world. Playing Barnsley at home may not be the most glamorous fixture to Sunderland fans at the SOL. How often it's taken for granted, the sheer quality of life when you can attend any game you like.

I'd be up around 9am, with no doubt a considerable level of alcohol swimming its way around my brain, yet I vow to join in with the celebratory football ban-ter called Soccer AM, on Sky TV. In between breaks and interruptions I visit the shower, don my football attire, drink copious amounts of English tea, whilst breaking into a Bacon sarnie. Then I'm ready. Ready to visit The Grange public house, which will expand the banks of my booze filled reservoir. Here merriment and jovial conversations are exchanged with the lads, the regulars, the diehards, the hardcore – Sunderland's friendly version of The Ultras.

From there it's a short hop on any of the buses making their way down Newcastle Road, towards the cathedral of football, the SOL. Then off the bus at the Wheatsheaf, via a programme seller (depending on whether or not I haven't already visited the Supporters Association shop in order to keep my copy pristine) thus joining in with a quick sprint, as a roar greets the two teams entering our great arena. Most likely one of the lads has ordered pre-match pints inside the ground, even though they taste like Grotbags' piss. These will be discarded halfway through, thanks to a second roar – the kick off roar and also the aforementioned bitter aftertaste. We then promptly arrive at our seats to cheer the lads on.

I can conclude that this would be a fair roundup of my typical match day routine.

Today though, I had no time to dwell on what could have been, or what has been. I'd only end up shedding a tear, especially today feeling vulnerable going to Afghanistan. The home game with Barnsley is the last thing on my mind. My four-month tour away from loved ones begins today. I suppose that's the biggest worry. Add to that the fear of the unknown and my stomach is aching with nerves. I've heard all sorts of horror stories, now it's my turn to go there. Are they true? What will happen? Will I come back? What will the missus do? Fuck, all these thoughts jostling for position in my brain. I think my head is about to explode. I pace the floor to calm down.

Everything is in order. All my bags are waiting for me in my converted Red and White bar in the shed. It'll be a long time before any drinks are enjoyed in here. Time gentlemen please, at least for four months anyway. I take a walk around the bar, eyeing the past memories, now engraved in photos. Again it feels like I'm being punished, sent to Siberia, like the Russians would have you believe, but then its no ordinary job I've got. Maybe that's all I strive for, to be ordinary. How the fuck did I end up in this shit state? I should be at home enjoying life, not concerned about if it will all end in the near future.

It's time to say goodbye to Angela, my wife. It is almost too unbearable to think about. I mustn't dwell on this too much, or I'll go to pieces. I could stare into her smile all day. I tell her I wish I could take her with me in my suitcase, she can hide in my tent, we'd be alright. Joking aside, I know she will be fine. I am though riddled with guilt, in the thinking that I brought her out to Cyprus, for a new life together and here I am, abandoning her in a foreign country, almost desolate over the winter months. I manage to find the words to this goodbye in the car, rather than the public eye of the air terminal. She's gone in a tormenting drift away, as our car reluctantly pulls off up the road back to my home. I head in the other direction, my feet under strict orders from my brain, to carry on regardless.

I'm to travel from Cyprus to Qatar and stay overnight there with the Americans. Not much chance of catching the evening kick off on Sky then? I won't be in the mood for sport anyhow.

I'm now sat at the end of my Hercules cargo aircraft, loaded with two military police dogs, both looking as miserable as me, complete with long faces and foam at their mouths. I feel dejected as my colleagues wave me off, the aircraft ramp slowly closes. The Mediterranean climate is shut out, in favour of a grey, cold, dark interior of the plane. There are two lads accompanying me, who are here to escort the dogs. They're off to Iraq. I don't know who is better off; the lads going to Baghdad, me, or the bleedin' dogs?

The flight to Qatar is dull, noisy and strange. Strange in the sense that I'm passing over such countries as Syria et al. Normally, I'd be keen on gazing out the window to see such delights as the Alps, at some stage of a usual plane journey on the way to some European destination in the sun. For now there would be the vast scale of the lunar-like landscapes of the Arabian Desert to stare out at.

Still I couldn't relax and read a book, never mind wonder about the state of play in the football. Sunderland would have kicked off by now, halfway through my flight. I bet I was the only Sunderland fan in the world that day on his way to such a random country as Qatar. I reached this Middle Eastern peninsula in darkness, both dazed and confused as to my bearings. Tiredness was a key factor playing on my mind and all I needed was sleep. It would be several hours before I was eventually to find some solace, in a forty-man tent, made up of bunk beds. This too was shrouded in darkness, as I tested my Cypriot phone sim card, to reveal the answer to my next question.

"2-0 2 Sunderland, Whitehead and Brown, hope ur ok luv u" preached the text message, acting as some kind of mental nutrient for the goodness of my mind. Well, Sunderland have three points to boost our climb up the table and my sim card works… well for receiving calls and texts at least.

On hearing the final score and our lasses' voice, via a call, I simply leaned back in my top bunk, pondering about life and how far I was away from home and my SOL. On that I drifted to sleep, only to be awoken by fucking Yanks performing their best renditions of Marine Corps ditties, whilst engaging in their morning exercise. Fuck that bollocks.

Sunday 22nd October 2006

Outside it was hot. Warmer than I expected, with a piercing sun unrepentant on my eyes as I swapped the black hole of the tent for brightness and light. It was as if I was a deep-sea creature, finally reaching the surface of the water. Most likely enhanced with the typical British facial expression of a blind mole squinting its way around the vicinity.

My aircraft was ready for departure, minus the dogs, thus resulting in a bark free zone. I was now in a surprisingly relaxed mood, as I sat lonesome down the back of the plane, staring out the windows, as we entered Afghan airspace. The pilots had been kind enough to sit me in the jump seat for take off out of Qatar; I suppose a kind of perk, when you are the only passenger. Still I wasn't really in the mood, but I accepted anyway.

As I sat alone, I remembered the hairy incident the day before over the skies of Iraq. I was seated alongside the window of the rear cargo door, when the haze of the low cloud base was set alight by radiating illumination, sparked by a flurry of anti-missile flares, sheared away from the aircraft to deter any heat seeking rockets fired from the ground. Were we under attack? This is the end before I've even arrived anywhere. I looked in shock at the other two dog handlers, hoping to see them reading a book, like nothing has happened, like this is an everyday occurrence on these flights. I was then somewhat alarmed to see them with the same amount of concern on their faces as I can only imagine was mirrored on mine. Eventually, the loadmaster on the aircraft came down to see us, reassuring everyone that it was simply a reflection of the clouds that had set this warning system into life. Thank God for that. Today there was no drama, just the dreary drone of the propeller engines.

We gradually fell to lower altitude after flying over Kabul and I knew I was on my way into some kind of hell…

Welcome to Kandahar, as my Hercules nose-dived to the floor, I was fully loaded with body armour and helmet. I simply thought "what the fuck am I doing here?"

as the two technician lookouts paved the way against missile attack. On touch-down, the cargo door opened to reveal mounds of dust projecting off the back of the four rotary engines.

Four figures came towards the tail of the aircraft to offload the explosive cargo on board. I recognised two of them from Cyprus, with one wearing a beaming smile, the size of the gaping desert itself. He was of course, the lad I was replacing and boy was he pleased to see me.

I'm whisked away to be shown around base. There are people jostling for position to add their input on the war situation passing through both my ears, as Chinook helicopters scarper over my head.

This is it son. This is Apocalypse again, never mind now.

Saturday 28th October 2006

It has been a few days since my last entry, mainly due to exhausting circum-stances. Days have surpassed the fifteen-hour mark, constantly grafting. Yester-day, I did find some light relief, only to end up lying in a hospital bed, dazed and confused as to what planet I was on. All this after one of my colleagues dropped a large forklift tine (which he was driving at the time) on top of my head, instantly splitting my temple, releasing spurts of claret red blood all over. Not that I knew what was happening. One minute an excruciating pain, the next trying to stagger up off the floor. Fuck me, a week in and I'm pissed already, or so I thought, eventually tuning in to the numbing effects of my head injury. With my first war wound under my belt, it was back to work. No time to lose, no manpower to replace me.

The incessant existence of Groundhog Day continually belting out tiresome hard labour was broken up by the fact that this was my first Saturday and with that a first match day in the desert. It has been a week now since arriving in this cesspit of a dump. It feels like I've been conscripted to a concentration camp, trudging around in endless grains of sand and dust, making the most basic of tasks that little bit more tiresome, making it extra work just to walk around here. You have heard of the phrase treading water, well replace the liquid with molecules of sand and I am only half way there in explaining how intense the suffering is.

My mind wandered from work, which didn't take much anyway, to my primary and favourite subject of football. A first league game at Hull's KC Stadium and that was all I knew. No build up, no hype, no media, no nothing. Thankfully, two TVs had been acquired before my time here and we would be treated with the services of Jeff Stelling and the boys on Soccer Saturday, when we had time. It's amazing the technology we have nowadays. There's me expecting Desmond Lynam and the vidiprinter out in this poverty stricken area, when instead we have the full latest offerings and exclusive footage, just like back home in the civilised world. Whilst at work there was the odd rumble of score updates over the forces' wireless, which were scrambled off radio sets inside of forklift trucks of all places. As you can imagine on a Saturday, one can witness a mad rush to secure a forklift with the only radio in – even if you can't drive the fucker.

And to that point, the workload had been the usual hectic, organised chaos, with no mention of the Hull City score. One of the other lads is a Tigers fan, so the score had better be good. I arrived in the lads' room (yes room, no tents, I'm impressed), as Jeff Stelling ran through the Premiership results. A fair cop, as that is the dominant league and openly deserves the full attention first in the pecking order. Why is it though, that the analysis takes far longer when you're waiting in vain for that one result? So it was frustrating when one of the boys commented on how we were "jammy bastards", leaving it until the final minute to score. Was it a wind up? No, as the Championship results were on soon enough for all to see, with Sunderland the 1-0 victors. It had been five minutes of agony, growing increasingly desperate to hear the final news.

Wallace in the last minute is quality, even more so the second yellow that followed for taking his shirt off when celebrating. Pure class, pure passion that's what we want to see, fortunately right at the end of play, too late for the dismissal to take any effect. I bet Keano wasn't too happy though, but official bragging rights belong to me at work.

Sunday 29th October 2006

Another fifteen-hour day of exertion, bullshit and bollocks was had. I don't mean to sound miserable, but when tiredness and apathy mix, expect a colossal explosion. The end result is a short temper and a monotone voice.

More war wounds were nearly inflicted, when pushing an aircraft pallet along a giant Airbus, it suddenly comes to a halt. My fingers were still travelling at speed, resulting in them becoming lozenged between the pile of pallets. Cue immense pain and the fear that if someone continues to push, I'm about to lose a digit. Thankfully, all ends well, as the hired Turkish crew and the lads prise my finger out and stick it in ice. God only knows what is going to happen next.

Monday 30th October 2006

To relieve myself from the everyday routine of work, I plant the seed of a moustache growing competition into the minds of the lads. In a light-hearted morale raising initiative, it'll provide a sense of bonding outside of military life. Fuck, look at me, I should be a psychologist. Inspired by the 1980s era of Falklands Veterans' taches, my hairy lip will take the form of footballing legends, obviously from that said era. Brought up on Everton by my father, yet changing allegiances to my hometown Sunderland, I have a choice of numerous players on which to base my tache. Do I go for a Bushy Mountfield, Prudent Hesford, Silky Agboola, Porn Harper or a Prim and Proper Heathcote? I suppose if I look like a consortium of all of the above, then that should be enough to see me win hands down.

Sanity arrives in the form of a parcel full of Sunderland Echoes, Football Echoes and my monthly glimmer of A Love Supreme. However, another thirteen hours inhaling dust, shit and all other roaming germs in the air await me first. Honestly, people in prison have things easier. It is weird out here, one minute slogging away in the confines of another Guantanamo Bay, the next there is a lull and a chance to sit in the sunshine, seemingly unreal that you are actually present in Afghanistan a war ravaged country and there I am relaxing engrossed in the two week old newspapers. I am currently wearing trainers, due to irritating blisters on my feet, a product of my new desert boots. Coupled with a bare chest and a camouflage sun hat, I feel this must make me look like a builder on a site, rather than someone belonging to the military.

The lads who have been here a while are constantly on a downer. Why can't Tony Blair and co pick a war with Tenerife, or somewhere idealistic like Iceland or somewhere exotic; the Maldives anyone? No, no, it'll be North Korea or Iran next on the agenda.

Tuesday 31st October 2006

It is Halloween today, but that doesn't mean a thing around here. To add to my woes, I've added a new injury to my list. I've managed to pull my neck muscles. As the day goes on I'm in agony, thus moving my body in the same direction as my head, looking like a robot.

It is my last day in trainers today, as I'm back in the usual attire of boots in the morning. My stylish look of a lager lout abroad is to be diminished. I shall miss this image, now fully tuned into military mode.

Often in times of rare quiet intervals, I wonder what it will be like when I return to civilian life. I am only accustomed to walking around like a zombie, in a state of depression, talking work and scraping the dust from my view. Will I ever be able to hold a normal, resolute conversation again? More alarmingly, will I ever be able to order another beer? The thought deepens my spirits.

Changing the subject, one of the lads has shown me the local massage parlour on camp, which is run by Russians, or some other Eastern bloc country. I shall be visiting soon, where hopefully I will ease my tension. Apparently the rules state that the suggestion of sexual extras will result in banishment back home in disgrace. Now I know what to do for an easy ticket home, not that our lass would be too impressed. It's not a bad story to tell down the local…

"Where did you say you had your first massage again?"

"In Afghanistan with the Russians," would come my reply.

It is these random experiences that keep you going through months of desperation.

After being promised a short shift of eleven hours, I was in a positive frame of mind with thoughts turning to Sunderland's up and coming midweek game at home to Cardiff. I was then immediately gutted to remember the four and a half hour time difference (in which we were ahead of Greenwich Mean Time), cue a 00.15am kick off time – bastards. A text alert from the old man would have to make do.

"Even in the early hours son?"

"Even in the early hours Dad," I instructed.

I wish I hadn't bothered.

I had drifted in and out of sleep; only to see the blue flash of my phone illuminate the four-man room… "2-1 2 Cardiff" left me riled all night, not getting a wink of sleep afterwards, cursing my team's luck. Oh well, another day in paradise to cheer me up followed.

NOVEMBER

Wednesday 1st November 2006

Day eleven in the big Kandahar house… and all is shit. I did find humour when stumbling across a postcard shop. I sent Afghanistan postcards home as a piss take. I bet not many people receive a postcard with local kids playing with bombs and rockets on the front. This was the high point of my day.

I once again unloaded the foreign Airbus, mindful of my finger situation, although the Turkish crew didn't bother to help us. Bloody dodgy bastards. I don't trust them after watching the film Midnight Express.

Thursday 2nd November 2006

I feel like a fraud ranting on in a tirade of complaints, after reading in The Sun about the recent experiences of The Royal Regiment of Fusiliers, funnily enough based up in the North East themselves. Apparently they were involved in running battles with the Taliban for 107 days. Fair play to those boys, massive respect.

If the SAS motto is "who dares wins", then I'm positive that the Kandahar motto must surely read "who knows, who cares?" as the whole place is as mad as a box of frogs. There are the Yanks, the Aussies, Estonians, Canadians, Dutch and more all vying for pole position, all thinking they are worthy of taking control of things.

Just to show how crazy the whole place is, when we eventually go to lunch, we see, for the second day in a row, those crazy Dutch bastards, patrolling the streets inside the safe haven of the camp. Now I don't know what they expect to find, or shoot, but we pissed ourselves, as the fuckers walked around as if they were in downtown Kandahar City. I reckon the whole region is about as far gone as my first shit.

I seriously consider the prospect of entering the famous desert marathon – the Marathon des Sables in which competitors endure a torturous twenty six mile run in dunes of talc-like sand, over seven days of the event. I'm not well read in marathons themselves, but after this four month sandy slog, I consider my training to have been thorough and better than those at home who go out running once or twice before doing the Great North Run.

Saturday 4th November 2006

Didn't even realise it was the footballing Sabbath that is Saturday. The days merge into one complete brain cluster out here. I don't finish until late, missing all the results, as the lads slump to another defeat at Norwich. My faith in Keano is unrepentant though and it's still early days yet. I keep telling the boys it's a marathon, not a sprint and to look at the table in May. They say I sound like a seasoned football pundit and more to the point, a broken record. How would I know, I've not seen any coverage to take notes.

Still football was put into perspective today, as mortars rained down on me as I pop my mortar cherry. It's unreal to think you are under attack. The air raid sirens have a modern feel to them since the haunting themes of the Second World War. However, the tones are just as scary, not knowing if one will land nearby, causing injuries and death. We are taught to wear our helmets and body armour. I simply roll over in bed, after all, what am I supposed to do if one of the fuckers lands on my head? Wearing such protective items would merely keep my body parts together, probably making identification of my remains a damn sight easier.

Sunday 5th November 2006

Fireworks night, tonight. Around here we will have to make do with flares only. It was a nightmare day today, receiving crap off everyone all day. It's a simple fact of life out here, that in these conditions, at some stage, everyone will snap.

I was offered the chance to visit the capital city, Kabul, for two nights today. It is a new venture to try and raise morale. On a rotation basis, two lads from Kandahar and two from Kabul will swap over, apparently giving the lads down south a break from the crippling work agenda, also allowing a drink or two in the various bars on offer in the capital's camp.

At first I agreed to travel tomorrow. Throughout the day, my knee jerk decision played on my mind, remembering past jolly trips that had turned horribly wrong, resulting in aircraft crashing or being shot down, in a needless loss of life. My good Corporal in charge of me swayed my decision to stay, adding that any operational trip in a war zone should be kept to a minimum. Why put my life in danger for a worthless task? All I could think about was Angie and how upset she would be if something did happen, when it could so easily have been avoided. At the end of the day, as soppy as it sounds, my wife comes before anybody; after all she is my best mate.

One of the group joked that I refused to travel because I was scared. Truth was he was right. Maybe not scared, just not daft enough to play along with a mad plan which could end up in tragedy.

Monday 6th November 2006

I sit at the end of the runway and watch the two volunteers take off for the higher climes of Kabul. The Hercules shoots for the sky, like a firework chasing the sun.

Meanwhile, back in reality, the two replacement Kabul lads have mucked in well. I did notice how fresh both of them appeared. When enquiring how long they had left to do (even the language sounded like prison speak) I was shocked to hear that both had only a few days left to serve. Both admitted how well they lived up there, quoting "a party every other night", which didn't go down too well with the inhibitors of this dry zone's exclusion from alcohol. They looked fresh, whilst we wandered around acting out Neanderthal caveman on acid scenes. They could not believe how harsh the working conditions were down here.

My mobile will not accept incoming SMS anymore, meaning I can only send blind text messages outbound. I feel a little lonely and isolated now our lass and I can't converse electronically.

Tuesday 7th November 2006

Not a bad day really. This must be due to me settling into a routine, or perhaps simply going through the motions, oblivious to the Kandahar craziness.

I even enjoyed a half hour break to engage in a mini-sunbathe, as off came my top to revel in the November sun. It is not often you can say that. If only they built a few decent hotels, swimming pools to boot, lifted the ban on alcohol and stopped bloody fighting, then Afghanistan would make a canny mint on the tourist industry – I'm serious.

There I was laid out, without a care in the world. I could have been in Ibiza or Las Vegas. But no, I was in a war zone with the enemy, or at least no man's land, situated a couple of hundred yards over the fence. Sunbathing as the forces' radio played cheesy summer dance songs, all I required was a lager and a pair of Speedos and it would have been like a perfect holiday. Normality was resumed with the arrival of more freight in an avalanche of dust.

I saw a shooting star tonight. I made the customary wish, but it wasn't connected with my current predicament. I should have been thinking about it, but then sometimes you should be careful what you wish for.

I had thought of things to write in view of today's entry, but my brain is on detox from reality, as I settle down for bed. The assumption that Groundhog Day awaits my arrival in the morning compounds my grief. I feel that sometimes I should just photocopy my notes; it would save me the punishment of writing about my day. Although then where would be the fun in that? It would be like using video referees to settle an argument in football. Where is the fun, the chance to moan, the option to argue?

Wednesday 8th November 2006

I awoke around half past three in the morning to what I thought was someone's warbled alarm clock. On gaining a state of full consciousness, I realised it was a station alarm, bellowing out across the base. Everything else was deeply silent, rigid to the core. The sound was akin to one of my cherished foghorns, rumbling in the distance, even if it did sound like it was on fast forward.

This process carried on for a further five minutes, finally slowing down, culminating to a standstill, reverting outside back to silence. I was curious as to what it was, but not overly concerned, especially so based on the lack of concern from the remainder of my room, all sleeping soundly. It did not seem like a warning. I simply shuffled along the corridor for a piss and squirmed around for half an hour before falling asleep.

On meeting the rest of my unit, it was revealed that there had been a mortar attack on the area. The alarm I had woken up to was the all clear signal. I had missed the main act, only catching the after-show party, having never heard the all clear sirens before. Thankfully no one was injured, only making a mess in one part of the camp.

I had a chuckle to myself today on the way back from one aircraft load. Riding on a set of large forklifts, travelling back to our works' tent, the local radio decided to play Summer Holiday by Cliff Richard. Surely somebody, somewhere, was trying to wind us up.

I finally crash into my room around 9pm. As I read through my collection of daily letters, an air raid siren hassles the evening's atmosphere. We are under attack for a second time in one day. I felt somewhat different to the way I did this morning. A slight discomfort in the knowledge that it could land anywhere, taking into the account of pot luck, accepting the idea that if it's your turn to go, then so be it.

No shells are heard on impact and the place resumes normality.

I did observe some freaks of nature earlier on this afternoon. One was the beautiful Monet skies, cast by a low sun, eloping for the night. Straight out of the film Vanilla Sky, the clouds were littered with pinks and purples, which brought a distant prospect of relaxation for ten minutes at dusk.

The other was a mini twister or tornado, caused by the thrust of the passing jet engines, sending a ripple through the dust, gradually building up speed, snaking and swerving towards us. There was never any element of danger, just a strange phenomenon, which excluded my thoughts from work for five minutes. Any form of entertainment that can supply such skills is a good thing in my book.

Saturday 11th November 2006

I have a good mind to visit my holiday rep. For starters the weather outside has been overcast all morning, followed by torrential rain and fork lightning. This has put a dampener on my four-month holiday. If only… back to reality and back to work.

The promise of a TV in our shambolic works' tent is on the horizon. Meanwhile, we graft all day, not knowing what time it is. I've stopped wearing my watch, as time goes quicker without it. I'm surprised to hear the final scores relaying over the radio then, as I presumed it was still too early. I was frustrated still, when the classifieds revealed both Sunderland and Southampton scored in a 1-1 draw. One of the lads took great delight in announcing that Gareth Bale, the little up-start with choirboy looks, had scored in the last minute for the Saints. I was past caring today, too tired for a response. Philosophically, what goes around comes around. The Hull lad would argue that's payback for the other week. I'd argue that we still avoided defeat.

In a break away from the game, today was Remembrance Day, not that we had the chance to pay our respects. We are too busy, even for fallen comrades, lest we forget in our own minds the untold sacrifices carried out for our country, in both distant and recent histories.

Sunday 12th November 2006

I find it quite amusing walking into the mess for dinner. You encounter all the stereotypical military characters of the Armed Forces.

In one corner the Special Forces lads, resplendent in their full on Grizzly Adams beards and North Face jackets, I find myself caught up in a four dimensional image of the Joy of Sex manual. I fully expect to see a hairy-bodied gentleman lying underneath a platter of grapes, secretly in wait for a fair maiden to breech his path.

The Taliban must sit in their caves and spot the buggers a mile off, clad in plain combat pants and black jackets, sponsored by The North Face from head to toe.

"Ah, there goes ze Special Forces again" (slightly German), chilling out in their pits.

Then come the Movers, complete with grim faces, heads bowed, sick as chips. Finally the office Chameleons, changing colour and mood to suit any higher ranked individual, over a course of cheese and biscuits. It does make me laugh.

Monday 13th November 2006

Today the hierarchy start to see sense; I go about drawing up a roster of days off, once every fortnight. After weeks of discussing the maybes and possibilities, we see some action at last. To say I'm as happy as a Mag in Greggs would be an understatement, as I've just found out that my first day off from this hellhole was on a Saturday. Back of the net. The routine and itinerary were now in the final planning stages and what a day it will be.

Wednesday 15th November 2006

Felt rubbish all day, as an onset of influenza has begun. My eyes are full of hot water, ready to close for a week or two. My head is dizzy; my limbs feel tired, inflicted with a sudden lack of energy. Welcome to the winter.

It all started yesterday afternoon as the darkest of clouds, which would have been the perfect tonic for the end of the world, appeared upon the horizon, moving at pace, adding a swirling sandstorm in there for good measure. It really did feel like Armageddon, the darkness descending, the winds picking up and the fork lightning choosing its velocity of voltage. I expected Superman to come beaming down with a plastic carrier full of discounted Kryptonite at any time.

Ever since then, the weather has been reminiscent of the UK, with Japanese earthquakes in the sky and heavenly napalm bombs. Needless to say the desert sand has transmuted into a muddy bog, insinuating scenes of World War trench life, as we rampage to the tents in a quagmire of piss rotten mud. At least it's a change from the Asthma inducing effects of the sun and the dust.

Thursday 16th November 2006

After yesterday's conclusion of the most recent weather forecast, which a Michael Fish/Sid Vicious lovechild would be proud to present, I can hereby add that the entire climatic conditions have definitely taken a turn for the worse.

I could close my eyes and imagine I was on Roker Pier, in the height of a North Sea Tsunami. This was proper Afghan dancing rain, pounding off the surface of one's skin, gnawing away at what soul and sanity was left residing inside.

The swamp that is our pan and cargo yard resembles a combination of Glastonbury, a builders' yard and a World War One battlefield, complete with trenches, timber and Portaloos, which are now starting to overflow.

Saturday 18th November 2006

Twenty-seven days later, one less than the film, but just as traumatic. I half expected a Thompson's holiday rep to knock at my door and provide the schedule for my day off. If there had been one, then this is what it would read...

The guest will enjoy the comforts of his bunk bed (top layer) until the ungodly hour of half ten in the morning. This will be enjoyed whilst listening to the Afghan rain bounce off the tin roof, as one's fellow workmates graft away.

The holidaymaker, after unanimously winning the King of the Tache competition, will thus shave the winning entry off and celebrate with a nice hot shower.

And then our facilities include a massage parlour (seriously), scheduled in for a visit at 12.30pm.

After the Eastern Bloc equivalent of Pat Butcher grinding out your wears and tears, the guest can enjoy a light bit of shopping via Pizza Hut and Tim Horton's (the Canadian Coffee and Doughnut chain) for a vanilla flavoured cappuccino, before the main event of the day.

Finally, sit and relax with a smuggled box of full bodied red wine, whilst enjoying the delights of watching one's football team claim three points in a 3-1 home win over Colchester United.

Maybe compared to a traditional pissed up night out, nowt to crow about. However, when considering you are near the Helmand province, adjacent to Kandahar, then it's not a bad day at all.

Sunday 19th November 2006

It was back to work and the familiar sound of rain battering down on our tin roof. Back to reality for me, still I had an extra half an hour in bed, which was appreciated. Perhaps swigging all that wine wasn't such a good idea. There was no hangover, just a little groggy feeling and a tad offbeat.

Saturday 25th November 2006

I write these words shivering from head to toe, my blood rapidly descending into ice. Outside it feels like Siberia and Hendon beach rolled into one, rather than Afghanistan. You just don't realise how cold it can get. Good job then I've landed an office job for the next few weeks, after putting my back out pushing heavy equipment around. The poor lads outside are freezing, whilst I'm now on my fourth cup of tea, yet my body still refuses to thaw.

My eyes feel as though someone has drawn a pencil around them. If I could paint a picture of how they feel, then I would probably compare them to one of those perforated strips of paper which tear off at the end of a letter. Tiny bits of holes surround my eyes, as they disintegrate away from my face.

I sit at my desk at work, scribbling away like Ebenezer Scrooge, hunched over my paperwork, shivering underneath layers of clothes that fail to keep out the ever biting cold. I had five layers of thermal clothing on, only for the Afghan chill to pierce its way through.

I decide to conform to technology and treat myself to an I-shuffle. Music is the way ahead in an attempt to keep me sane and guide my inner soul through the long winter nights. I shall be downloading my soundtrack to war tonight. No songs belonging to Radiohead or Sinead O' Connor, they have no place here. Purely upbeat tunes will suffice.

As DJ Danny Tenaglia preaches… Music is the answer.

It was a 1-1 draw at Wolves last night. I had no chance of catching the game, which was rather frustrating, seeing as it was live on the telly: the supposed grudge battle between Messrs McCarthy and Keane, not that I saw any of the expected over the top hype from the press. How is it that anywhere one goes in the world, if your team is playing in that time space, you're bound to bump into an opposition fan? In this case it was Winston, the Wolves die-hard and alleged member of the Wolves Subway Army hooligan outfit. And no, he's not the stereotypical black man I was expecting. In fact he's white, his nickname deriving from his surname – Churchill. At least it was honours even, as I'd done myself no favours, ribbing Winston beforehand at any opportunity. Obviously, through his golden Wolves spectacles, they deserved to win, with only a deflected Stephen Elliott goal sharing the spoils.

Me: "Sign of a good team though Winston."

Winston: "What's that?"

Me: "Playing shit and still getting a result."

Winston: "Bollocks, you're going nowhere pal."

Monday 27th November 2006

Nothing of note happened today, apart from the ironic, comical scene of four of us playing the tactical war game Risk, during a slow night shift. It is a board game, where each of the players controls their army and battles it out to rule the world. Here we are in the middle of Afghanistan, playing toy soldiers. I wonder if this is how the United Nations resolves its disputes behind closed doors. I can just picture it now, George Bush and Tony Blair on one side, the French and Russians last to be picked for any side, à la school team selection process, on the other, kicking up a stink.

Of course as sod's law would predict, which country do I pull out of the hat to invade... bloody Afghanistan.

The night was quiet, leaving me time to download tunes to my new toy, ranging from Simple Minds' Belfast Child to Bad Manners' Samson and Delilah and from the premises of Hey Matthew to giddy pop in Erase/Unwind. I find a mate's laptop full of forgotten goodies, from many indiscriminate dance floors, of various genres, from which to plunder my morale-boosting synergy of songs.

I received a few parcels both yesterday and today off my Mam, aunty and mates back home. It really is mad the amount of mail I receive, all greatly welcomed. I did allow myself a laugh at the fact some "precious classified" material arrived from a UK inbound flight, nestling in with my contingent of personal parcels. It was a battered cardboard box, nothing flash, although its contents were a bundle of American Dollar notes in excess of $500,000.

It looked the part for me, safely nurtured with my own mail. I considered hiring a pilot who worked for one of the local Azerbaijani freighter airlines. We would jet off over the Afghan Alps, into a whole new world of sinister proceedings. It wouldn't last long though with our lass at the helm.

Tuesday 28th November 2006

I received a Christmas tree in the post today. I had declared that the festive period would be cancelled this year, thus being replaced by a mythical month with a new name. What could be a good alias for a new month in our calendar? Ah yes, Kandember, yeah that sounds good. It will resemble a chilled month, that has no bank holidays, no extra shopping hours, with all aspects of fun completely out-lawed. The month will remain in a thirty-one day cycle, where the food in season will send the unfortunate souls into a state of hibernation, as the mind switches onto autopilot. In short – Christmas is cancelled.

The only positive aspect to arise from this new monthly development is in the form of first birthdays for my mam and brother-in-law, Andy. Knowing my Mother she will be well pleased with her first birthday, although I worry about her first day in nursery.

Before I sign off from night shift, I decide to revel in a liquid breakfast of Cherry Brandy and Coke, rapidly changing into the Vodka variety. Happy days.

Wednesday 29th November 2006

It's now the small hours of Wednesday as I write this. Today, or rather yesterday, is a day to forget. I hang my head in shame, as for the first time in my twenty seven year old supporting career I admit to the fact that I didn't even realise that Sunderland were playing a match. There, it wasn't so bad to admit it. I feel like a drug addict relieved to reveal their addiction to an audience. I do cite mitigating circumstances, due to my location, lack of sleep and incessant mental torture.

I vow to stay up though as punishment and say three hail Mary (Melvilles), as I catch The Lads' result away at Loftus Road, QPR, on the midweek Soccer Special. There I am seated in a darkened room, most likened to a photo laboratory, earphones in place to watch the constant updates without disturbing the other three lads, who are enjoying their rest in the land of nod.

I'm rewarded with a 2-1 win, thanks to strikes from Daryl Murphy and Grant Leadbitter. Now we motor, now we motor. Watch out Premiership.

I celebrate once again with a breakfast of Cherry Brandy and Guinness. Quality.

My mood was also improved upon the arrival of a personal welfare box, sent out by our lass. The contents were amazing. Pots of caviar, duck and goose pate, Chilean merlot, and a selection of various ports, you can't ask for finer tastes than that.

KANDEMBER

Friday 1st Kandember 2006

Alas, it's the first day of a new month, in fact the very newest of months – Kandember. I have been given an advent calendar for the Stone Age month of December, but for me that is a step back in time. Seriously though, I may still use the gift, albeit as a motivational tool to count down the number of days until my return home on a week's R and R, otherwise known as rest and recuperation. I find that if I break my remaining sentence down into sections, then my days out here seem few, well almost. The calendar dates are around the corner, within touching distance, yet they seem further away than ever.

I am starting to become paranoid about the showers in the block. The water here has a tendency to completely switch off after they have been used at breakfast time. This means if you are on night shift, you wake up later to find the cleaning facilities rather temperamental. I begin my crazy rendition by popping along to see if the showers have any water, then returning complete with towel and toiletries. Back in civilisation I would wash my hair first, working down the body. Here, I begin with the crack of my arse, purely down to the sole reason that if the water cuts out in an instant, at least my bum hole will have been refreshed, leaving no skid marks that Brands Hatch would be proud of on the back of my towel.

Saturday 2nd Kandember 2006

Forget football, I've had four and a half hours sleep for no reason, thanks to lack of man-management at work. Somehow, somewhere I hear in the distance that we've beaten Norwich 1-0 at home, but it means nothing to me in my state of delirium. Don't even know who scored. What's going on with my life?

Sunday 3rd Kandember 2006

Ah, 'tis Murphy who scored. Phone calls home can be informative, but they are always treasured and rewarding.

Wednesday 5th Kandember 2006

After watching a batch of Trigger Happy TV the comedy sketch series, I felt mischievous myself. Hence when one of the lads foolishly fell asleep during night shift, adjacent to a permanent marker, he was clearly asking for trouble. After colouring his nose tip black, three whisker markings on either cheek promptly followed, the lads now pissing themselves with laughter. Little did he know he was now a fully-fledged member of the Black Cats.

I then continued in this midnight madness and asked someone to cut a Mohican style hairdo into my head, purely to wind the hierarchy up, who by now had dispersed for a coffee. I only revealed the full extent of my outlandish cut on shift handover, to a barrel of laughs, which in the end is what it is all about – keeping spirits up, in this mundane existence of eat, sleep, shit, work.

I will have the last line of hair removed later… after all; it isn't even straight.

Friday 8th Kandember 2006

I am on my fourth coffee in fifteen minutes, sat shivering in the works tent. The lads are outside in the bitter ice rink. I hibernate into my I-shuffle. Bring on a bit of Billy Idol or Martine McCutcheon; yes you heard correct. It reminds me of Sunderland's First Division, record-breaking title success, back in the day, circa 1999. Kevin Phillips had just sealed the title with a stunning curler to make it 3-1 at Barnsley. It was a joyous time on Wearside, real hope and expectation took control of the City, under the silver lining of the club's first promotion at the SOL.

It was also a fantastic and exciting era personally for me. I had started life at University, met our lass and held down a quality job as a chef in a family pub.

Everything in life was magic, no worries, plenty of friends, a great girlfriend and awesome football team to match. I sat at the bar surrounded my family, friends and acquaintances glued to the promotion celebrations at Oakwell, sipping Lambtons, when Sky TV aired the end of programme credits, in which highlights of the match are accompanied by a tune, a testament of those times and a summary of the game. It was of course McCutcheon's Perfect Moment and no other song could sum up my feelings at that time. It also adds a touch of winter warmth to the Afghan cold, leaving me curious as to where the years disappear to and the good times to boot. How did I go from there to here at this present moment right now. What am I doing here? The niggling all too familiar feeling of aching bones and a cracker bread throat disrupted my audio enjoyment, resulting in a cacophony of irritation as man flu knocks at my door.

"Knock, knock," comes a stern voice.

"Hello, who's there?" I ask.

"A bout of man flu for you Sir," offers the hallucinogenic butler, without remorse.

"Fuck off man flu, I don't need your shit just right now," I plead.

"Tough bollocks," replies man flu. "Deal with it. You are in Kandahar in Kandember, what do you expect? What do you want, a medal?" tortures the voice within my head.

"No… I want a fucking Knighthood, putting up with this torment," I offer.

And with that, resources of medication are taken, to prevent anymore torturous mind confrontations.

Saturday 9th Kandember 2006

True enough, some kind of flu has hit the camp again. Not man flu, or any of your pussy head colds, this is the real knock yer off yer feet strain, possibly fatal if untreated. And yes muggins has the symptoms. Feels like someone's grated my brain and made bolognese out of my spinal chord. A trip to the medical centre is on the cards. No energy to write. Don't know what's going on, as hallucinations, an outbreak of sweats and the Ricki Lakes (shakes) take hold, whilst vast amounts of lung butter congeal at the back of my throat, ready for dispatch.

Football is in my head, something to do with a dream involving the film Escape to Victory, or am I seeing things again?

Tuesday 12th Kandember 2006

I feel as though I've awoken from the flu slumber party now. I do though still suffer the body tremors and aftershock of the initial virus. Apparently Sunderland won again, 2-1 against Luton Town, but as yet it's unconfirmed. I'm still putting my life back together after the crazy happenings of recent days.

In the midst of my flu-induced fabrications, I came face to face with my brother-in-law, Andy. I recall it being around about last Sunday, bizarrely bumping into him. He himself is in the Army and was here for a fleeting visit. It was good to see a friendly face, if a touch unreal. I have rarely seen him in a military environment in the past and so to see him now, in a region of conflict was madness, only adding to my fragile state of mental bliss.

Wednesday 13th Kandember 2006

I find myself receiving sharp pains in the temple, combined with a severe tightening of my skull. Then it happens. I explode into the Incredible Hulk, having serious fits of rage at various people around work. Only when I sat down, did I realise that I was slowly going insane. My eyes feel strained and a total lack of energy flows over my body. What the hell is going on?

I am constantly tired and without regard for work anymore. I am even snappy on the phone back home to our lass and I can't help it. I feel awful afterwards, maybe it's a nervous breakdown.

There was an Afghan national airline parked up the road, next to the civilian air terminal. It appeared to be their version of an internal flight, much like our own easyJet or RyanAir, reminding me of normality back home. Examples like this, which have the slightest connotations of home linked to it, are driving me nuts.

You can imagine my delight when I was tasked with carrying nine Afghan army soldiers' coffins off the back of a Hercules. With their families watching and weeping for their loved ones, I was transfixing my mind to a place far, far away, or I would have cracked. These unfortunate souls had served their country well, at least playing their part in the long restoration of their country. And that is what it is all about, why we are here I suppose. These were the unlucky ones, but they will say they didn't die in vain if their homeland is returned to peaceful ways.

As we finally finished this unwelcome task, a Romanian executive plane taxied past, with one of their VIPs on board. Imagine their horror, peeping out of their porthole window to see a flurry of coffin boxes. I am surprised the jet didn't turn around and take off again.

Thursday 14th Kandember 2006

A strange day, even for Kandahar's standards. Today I star in a Christmas pantomime, then stroll around in mid-winter drinking iced cappuccinos. Is this really Afghanistan? There is no in between in this place. From one extreme to the other, happiness to depression, tears to laughter. I have even begun to check the sky above every day. I check to see if there is a sun and a moon, reassuring myself that I am on the same planet as the rest of the human society. I keep believing that Jeremy Beadle or Dom Joly are to appear at any moment, armed with a crew of cameramen and sound recorders, declaring the whole scenario one big joke, an experiment to see how long we'd last. We were, I'm convinced, in a state of the art recording studio, somewhere near Hemel Hempstead, rather than Afghanistan.

The Sun newspaper is in town; well the RAF photographers are on their behalf, here to record the arrival of the tabloid's gift boxes to the frontline troops, a tradition to mark the coming of the festive period. The bosses asked for two willing volunteers to dress up as Santa Claus and pose in numerous photos to be printed in the media. No one was keen, so I stepped forward, if only for a laugh and some light relief from the routines of work. Two hours in total it took, there I was suited and booted posing as Father Christmas, forgetting my Kandember principles for today, only I've never seen Father Christmas holding an SA80 rifle before. For the first time out here, I was shot at… thankfully only with a massive paparazzi style camera lens.

Today made me think, the art of war may not be a bad place to be after all. I decided to compile a small list of things to do, should I need to come back a second time.

Moustache Competition – As tried and tested this time out, however hide everyone's razor, to see the full effects.
The Poo Pond Dare – To compliment the delights of the barren desert, Kandahar camp also includes the quality facility of its own sewerage system; after all we need to be self-sufficient out here. The nickname of the sewage works is the originally named Poo Pond. Depending on the direction of the wind, one can go

to bed at night with the unpleasant taste of shite in one's gob. A real shitburger to munch on for bedtime supper. It is basically one large open lake, with logs swishing around and other things I dare not imagine. To add a bit of spice, perhaps a dare consisting of who can last the longest at the side without vomiting, or who can jump in the deepest, could be concocted. The dare of who can swallow the most chod would surely be going too far.

Runway Dare – This time, a taunt to see who can shuffle the closest to the side of the main runway, when a gigantic C17 cargo plane is rolling into take-off speed. The lads and I had an initial trial at night the other week, with us all requiring a swift change of underwear afterwards.

Secret Santa, Kandahar Market Style – Finally to round things off, why not use the festivities as an excuse to wind your mates up, buying them shitty gifts and then making them try them out. For instance this year, I have bought my nominated person a talking toy parrot, in which I have recorded expletives, then complementing this derisory present with an ounce of good old Texas chewing tobacco, in a bid for him to woo some American officer cowboy, spitting dark bile everywhere.

Saturday 16th Kandember 2006

Just endured an eighteen-hour slog of a shift in the biting Afghan cold. I could probably handle a North or South Pole crossing, after experiencing the winter here. It really does numb you into just wanting to cuddle up and go to sleep – which is dangerous, especially considering the temperature and wind chill is now past minus twelve degrees. The weather tricks the body into a mental shutdown, slowly eating away at the sanctuary of your soul. It's mind over matter, dog eat dog, don't let nature grind you down. Mother nature? More like motherfucker nature – she's a right bitch.

I have no energy, still sapped by disease, weather and fatigue. Good news though on the football front. Despite being two goals down at Burnley, we snatched a point in stoppage time. I had heard the half time score via our new TV hastily positioned in the crew tent. It came as a nice surprise when the radio commentator announced "Burnley 2, Sunderland…….2" over the wireless. That'll do, that's the spirit. Compliments to David Connolly.

Wednesday 20th Kandember 2006

Happy Birthday to my Mam and brother-in-law, yesterday. They will be delighted at missing out on getting a year older, with this year not counting in the record books, being the stipulated month of Kandember. It is entirely reminiscent of people who are born on the leap year date of the 29th February.

I help celebrate their day, supping a can of Guinness, trying to unwind in my room. I can't help but watch the music channels on offer, constantly churning out Christmas hit after hit. One minute it's Wham's Last Christmas, the next it's The Pogues' Fairytale in New York. This cements my miserable feelings, longing for the return to the days of the works' party, or an all day session with our lass, starting with fajitas, pitchers of beer and shooters in Jonny Ringo's in Sunderland city centre, concluding at Brogan's bar, hours later.

I feel empty inside, like someone has invented a human Dyson hoover and sucked away my spirit and soul. It is a horrible feeling.

Anyway it's Mam's birthday and so I raise a plastic cup to my old dear, wishing her many happy returns.

Friday 22nd Kandember 2006

Morning men, starboard at ten. Hands off cocks and on your socks.

Christmas is slowly creeping up, as the Hits channel in our room continues to belt out carols, tunes and rhymes, all festive, all depressive. However, after bumping into celebrity chef Gordon Ramsay the night before, spirits were high amongst the lads. Like a sad bastard we had photos and autographs, with one of my all time non-football heroes. The missus then revealed over the phone that she had bought Ramsay's autobiography for me for Christmas. That same book which was wrapped up in my room, by any chance? Bastard. I'd settled for a scrap piece of paper, which looks doubly crap, as my pen ran out, whilst Gordon wrote. All I need is my football hero Paul Gascoigne to pass through now, to complement Gordon's visit. Fair play to the culinary master, coming to visit the troops, days before the festive season. He even obliged with one of the lads recording a video of Ramsay on his phone, with a special Christmas message for his Dad.

"Merry Christmas Keith…. now fuck off." Cue fits of laughter all around. A true legend indeed.

Back home the news is dominated by the freezing fog causing travel chaos, with the usual moaning and slagging off about the transport system. Whinging fuckers.

On a lighter note, we play Palace on Sky tonight, entwined with the usual nightmare kick off time. The game ends at 2am, with me up at 6am to start my twelve hour shift – not good. To get me in the spirit of the match, I enjoy the odd can or three of the black stuff, swiftly followed by a selection of port, which has been smuggled in for Santa's arrival. All five mini bottles are necked, leaving me to shout the odd expletive in a fit of football Tourette's, as others try and sleep. Alcohol tends to be more lethal when not consumed for a while. Drink is banned here, for security and safety reasons, mainly due to troops carrying their own personal weapons, complete with rounds.

Despite dominating the game at Helhurst, our bogey team somehow score and win 1-0, to my disgust. I wake up late, sleeping in. Not a good idea for the future, but it's Christmas after all.

The wheels have come off Keano's rescue attempt, but I still have no clue where we are in the league, thanks to me being inebriated when Sky flashed the league table up on screen. Even past editions of the Echo have not arrived yet due to the grand scale of demand on the forces' postal system.

To hide my alcohol breath at work, I downed half a tub of garlic chutney, sent out to me in a food parcel by my sister. I reckon this pissed the bosses off even more than the alternative stench of booze, or as the Yanks here call it, liquor. Fucking pop to you and me Northerners.

Monday 25th Kandember 2006

Merry bloody Christmas, yer bastards. I received a Sunderland calendar to help me count down the days. I see Ben Alnwick – our first choice keeper at the beginning of the season - is in, even though he's off to Spurs in the January transfer window. I open a letter to read that some first team players have been playing threes up with a lass back home, with a video doing the rounds as well. Can't see Keano having that going on at his club. Suppose that'll be even less players on me calendar.

I go to take a shower, but there's no running water. We then have to queue for over half an hour in the shitty drizzle, for our stone cold Christmas lunch, complemented by frozen sprouts. Depressed is not the word. I find new depths to sink to. All I think about is what folks back home are up to. This frame of mind isn't helping.

I'm too ill to write anymore, thanks to Billy Vodka and his mates, from yesterday.

Tuesday 26th Kandember 2006

A day to remember and for all the positive reasons. Our section have been cordially invited along to participate in a 5-a-side football tournament, on camp in a place known as the Boardwalk. It's a recreational area, which houses a host of temporary eateries such as Burger King and Pizza Hut – a holiday camp, I hear you cry. It's an enclosed playing area, with the food establishments and various bric-a-brac shops running around the square perimeter. A kind of food court-cum-shopping centre if you like. Inside the courtyard there lies a Canadian portable ice rink, a stage for any proposed concerts and a makeshift football pitch, as only makeshift will suffice for the Brits, as usual.

This was a 5-a-side tournament which would involve a series of group matches to determine the winner. As it meant an afternoon away from work, a lot of the lads were interested. For me I would have attended, even if it fell in my stand down time. Playing football is a release, a break away from all our troubles, wherever you are in the world. This particular scenario was no exception. So we dragged our sorry arses down to the Boardwalk, in rather surreal weather for this time of year. For once the Afghan winter took pity on us, wore its shades and treated us to an afternoon of pleasant warmth. Our team was a combination of veteran playmakers and raw youthful energy, maybe lacking skill, but no ounce of drive. Being where we were meant many of the team didn't have the basic football kit, in which we would perform every week, still thinking we can do a job for England. So the likes of Gucci white boots made way for Silver Shadow flimsy Hi-Tech trainers and shiny shin pads, swapped for… well, fuck all. I didn't even have any footy socks, so opted for none at all, referring to a John Barnes/Zola Budd lovechild inception. Many resorted to digging out whatever they could lay their hands on, resulting in an amalgamation of colours, styles and comedy value. Passing allied nations watched on in disbelief, joining in with the banter.

I opted for the red and white cloth of Sunderland, thus spreading the word once more of the North East's biggest team. The rest of my clobber was made up of a pair of holiday swimming shorts and an outer top layer of a classic retro Umbro style training top. I looked like I'd just been 'pimped my ride' by a collaboration of TK Maxx and Oxfam.

The pitch left a lot to be desired, as jagged lumps of granite glistened from within the earth's crust, in order to let one know that nature was the referee here. Even Cristiano Ronaldo would hasten to go down on a whim here. The ball – a plastic shell like acrylic effort (as the PT flight wouldn't hand out their best balls, understandably) complimented the surface on which it would be played, deciding to fizz and whip off any pebble or rock lying in its wake. The biggest highlight out of this rogue line up were the two goals themselves. Ingeniously created out of aircraft cargo nets, wrapped around a wooden frame structure. Then the corner flags were created in celebration of classic British subtlety, in the fact that they were indeed warning signs, claimed from other (mainly American) parts of the camp. It's slightly weird taking a corner next to a sign reading "No Smoking within 500 ft." Yet where there's a will…

In the end, my team came second, remaining undefeated, without conceding a goal, but only scoring one. A record I'm sure king of mundane, Sven, would be proud of. However, it wasn't about the performances, it was about the social enjoyment, camaraderie and micky taking, which I think football generates in unique abundances. Spirits were up again, only an after match pint and finger sandwiches required now… I wish.

I'll always remember though the day the lads and I performed football ballet with a bunch of rocks, in the middle of Afghanistan, on a Boxing Day in the sun. You can keep your dip at Seaburn.

In all the excitement, it was nearly forgotten that there was a full football fixture list on offer back home. Sunderland welcomed Leeds, as they did two years earlier the last time we were promoted under McCarthy. Another bumper crowd as is the norm on this calendar day, this time they trundled home enjoying a home win. What I'd give to be with them rather than here. Still, it's cracking with the banter exchanges when my club enjoys attendances of over forty thousand. The lads have no comeback to that fact. They may mock the team, or take the pee out of our recent Premiership form, but when the subject turns to support, Sunderland are second to none. Two goals to none against dirty Leeds and we are on the march again.

Saturday 30th Kandember 2006

I awake to a blaze of news headlines surrounding the execution of Saddam Hussein. This will be a poignant chapter in history and a sad reminder of one of the reasons why we are all here, to stamp out terror worldwide.

Sunderland's final game of the year ends in defeat. I kind of expected it, after catching glimpses of Sky's pre-match news, declaring that North End haven't won on Wearside in something like forty odd years. This put the mockers on from the start. Couple that with Preston becoming a bogey team, strangely play-ing our own Tommy Miller in midfield. They win 1-0 and the man the media are pissing their pants over, David Nugent, scores. Happy New Year it is, then. Still my weeks R & R is waiting like a blind date behind Cilla's screen, in anticipation of a trip away for seven days. I'll pick… and it's Cyprus. I'll be back just in time to enjoy one of my favourite periods of the season – the FA Cup Third Round weekend.

JANUARY

Monday 1st January 2007

Only three days until I leave this hell hole for a week recuperating, and Sunderland help me on my way, climbing into the top half of the league at last, dancing by Leicester City, 2-0. The boy Connolly is on fire at last. Keep this up lads and we might have a chance of the play-offs, either Wembley or Cardiff, we don't care.

Thursday 4th January 2007

I have re-entered civilisation. A new world, with trees, roads, people, smiling faces and more. It's almost unreal. A cruel virtual reality perhaps? Travel five and a half hours and I'm not on the same planet, surely?

I'm lucky to be here, being honest. My original aircraft had been delayed, which has become the norm, unfortunately with RAF aircraft. Fate came to my rescue, as out of the blue, another airframe saved the day, allowing me to arrive home in Cyprus on time. Open the Red and White Tractor.

Saturday 6th January 2007

Back home, back in comfort, as I sit, can in hand, watching the delights of Soccer AM. I'm like a kid in a sweetshop. There is a whole range of football on the box, as our lass goes mad to see the channels flicking from Football Focus to Soccer AM, to Teletext, akin to a football video jukebox, thus playing all the right tunes to me.

Spit, my good friend and neighbour, is here to join in the fun. He's expecting his first child – a boy, any day now, so I've agreed, tongue in cheek, that whoever scores in the Sunderland game today and the Spurs match tomorrow (he's a Lilywhite) will go down as the middle name of his baby. This theory goes tits up after Sunderland are beaten 1-0 at Preston, by a Brett Ormerod goal.

"We're not having that in his name," came the response.

So that is a grand total of two cup games played this season and not one goal scored. Still, we'll hide behind the old adage of concentrating on the league. Hopefully we won't see Preston again this season. Our lass tries to wind me up by ringing my brother-in-law, Al, who is at the match. She only goes and rings him in stoppage time, to see if the lads look good for snatching an equalizer, obviously frustrating for me because I don't want to know, saving myself for the delight of confirmation through the classified scores. Besides, she's disturbing the poor lad at the match in a crucial climax.

And that was that. My home football entertainment over until I finish my tour. It could have been slightly more exciting to be honest. Overall in the 2006/07 season the aggregate score against North End reads Preston 6 Sunderland 1. Not great reading against one of the big guns in the league.

Still, we are merry with wine, whilst we all reminisce about my journey home from Kandahar. This involved me insisting on being half cut flying out of that war zone, for fear of being shot down. If I was going out in a fireball of glory, then I was going out worse for wear, oblivious to pain. Little did the hierarchy know I had a sly bottle of Jack Daniels tucked away in my pocket whilst working. I even went to the lengths of covering my booze breath with sachets of malt vinegar, fresh from the British mess. All good fun.

Monday 8th January 2007

Time back in Cyprus is slipping away like Afghan grains of sand slipping through my fingers. Soon I will have to return to war. I remember once trying out a parachute course. They said the second jump and not the first would be the hardest, as you know what is coming the second time around. I can safely say, the same can be said for my journey back. My biggest fear was that of the unknown, with my anxiety matched in some proportions with obscure excitement. This time, I know what to expect, the negatives involved in separation from my wife. This will be the longest flight of my life.

Meanwhile back on Earth, I find myself developing strange dreams. Perhaps it's the dread of my impending return. Last night I dreamt of waking up from my bunk bed in Kandahar. My four-man room is empty, so too the block, my assumption being that everyone must be at work. I carry on with my daily grooming routine and step outside to see if anyone is about. The whole scene is of a deserted desolated area, no one around, the wind rustling through the air, abandoned Land Rovers and Jeeps, derelict in the road. Everyone has gone home. They have forgotten me, I'm left behind. It is at this stage, I wake up in a panic, my heart racing, so pleased to see our Angela's bemused face next to me. I really must get a grip.

Friday 12th January 2007

I'm sat at Brize Norton, in Oxford, nursing a hangover from last night. It's not too bad, a mere dull headache that lurks behind the eye sockets, ready to pounce when my pupils catch a glimpse of daylight. This is the main reason why I'm sitting in my mate's room, with the blinds down, as the rain half-heartedly glances the window, just to reassure me that I am in England. I'm sure this particular region has its own rain cloud.

My head is still spinning, not at all to do with the drink, but the sheer dizzy concept of being in Cyprus one minute, dozing in and out of sleep, squashed between two squaddies the next, then chatting away to lads I've never seen for ages over a cup of tea in Hanover, Germany, during a stop off. I then survive a take off, bombing around in crosswinds of over 40mph, grabbing my bags on arrival in the UK, whisked away to get changed, finally sat in front of a good old English pint in the local pub.

My brain is still recovering from the first stage of my tour in Kandahar; my body feels like it is in Cyprus, meaning my feet are wobbling back in Blighty. I am certainly in the frequent flyers club now. It is not only the travelling to take into account in the factors of fatigue. All the emotions of further goodbyes to my wife, which have become no easier, people wanting to say hello: "how are things over there?" What do you think? I find myself becoming mixed up in both past and present conversations, talking nonsense to mates, thinking I am finishing off the same patter I was chatting away to them two hours ago. The reality is they were months ago, and people have moved on since then.

I was planning on a quiet night in tonight, to aid my constant tiredness, ready for my flight back to Afghanistan tomorrow. That plan has been instantly put to bed, as I receive a phone call off my long lost friend Killa, ordering me out for a pint.

Monday 15th January 2007

My first chance to record anything of note. I arrived back in Afghanistan in the early hours of Sunday morning. Since then I've been playing catch up with sleep, as I recover from two nights on the piss back in the UK, a four and a half hour time difference plus the routine tiring effects of travel.

I remember flying back from Cyprus to Brize Norton in Oxfordshire, via Hanover in Germany, spending two days in England, before catching a connecting flight back out to Afghanistan. Apparently Michael Palin is looking for work elsewhere, after my travelling exploits of recent times.

It was touch and go that we made it back to Kandahar. A series of delays to our Tri Star aircraft caused a twenty-four hour delay, not that I was complaining, at least I could catch a glimpse of that day's football.

I was slightly aghast when the aircraft captain spoke over the intercom to personally thank the eagle-eyed passenger who spotted a screw loose on one of the wings. I took it all in good spirits, believing the pilot to be participating in jovial banter in a bid to relax everyone before a nervous flight. However, when a maintenance vehicle pulled up at the side of the plane, I was searching for the Jack Daniels. Tough shit though - I had none.

Finally, an eight hour flight was endured, then collecting my limited bags and waiting for the sim card to register on the local network, yes, Afghanistan has a local mobile system. It was only then did I see that we had beaten Ipswich 1-0 at the SOL, with that boy Connolly on the score sheet once more. I can't emphasise again, just how much this can raise my mood, even if I'm severely depressed to be back in this concentration camp. I feel like a battery hen, but at least one that supports Sunderland, who in turn are looking buoyant for the play-offs. Give me Wormwood Scrubs anytime.

Tuesday 16th January 2007

Now the final stretch is on, I bide my time with winding some of the Army seniors up. We have all been detailed to wear headwear (a normal requirement in any military establishment, however often relaxed in high octane areas such as here). I rely on my old faithful winter issue Russian hat, which for some reason, even though I have been given permission to wear it, still offends many Army hierarchy, who like to stick rigid to their Berets. I have been wearing the woolly garment with the flaps hanging down over my ears, designed to keep my lugs warm. Apparently I'm wearing the said item in the wrong manner, being told to "sort your hat out lad" a number of times, in strict disciplinarian seventies manspeak.

I do feel like pointing out that we are in the confines of a war zone and surely there must be more important issues on the agenda than the state of my hat, obviously not. Anal is not the word, it is far beyond that. If we're gonna die, it's clearly imperative we look our best.

Wednesday 17th January 2007

I awake to the sound of not too distant gunfire. I was told last night that the Taliban were close to claiming nearby Kandahar City. It is definitely kicking off around here; I can sense it in the air.

Thursday 18th January 2007

Turns out that the rattling of rifle rounds I heard the other night was the local Afghan forces on a training exercise. So much for my senses!

Saturday 20th January 2007

Tired beyond belief today. My eyes are stinging as though someone has rubbed them with sand; such is my irritation of fatigue.

I do though manage to pull myself together after work, as Vaughny and I watch the room TV to ourselves (for a change) as the afternoon's fixtures unfold before us. It's Sheffield Wednesday today and as expectation grows in the North East, I receive news from home that over 6,000 Mackems are on the road to Hillsborough. I long for days like these. The days where towns and cities are swamped with red and white in every corner. Every pub has a marra, a mackem in every chippy, everywhere you turn there's one of us. I can only imagine the immense feeling of pride and satisfaction at the sight of home fans simply in awe of our mass cult following. You display your tribal colours, chanting terrace tunes, head aloft, shoulders upright to attention. The noise, I'm sure, is overwhelming.

My fears were that the lads would flatter to deceive in a show of stage fright in front of the massed ranks, like most bumper Boxing Day performances. Dwight Yorke started proceedings, drilling in a shot. Cue celebrations in my room as Carlsberg goes everywhere. I'm only on my second illicit can when Hysen makes it two on half time. "We're on our way, we're on our way" reverberates off the corrugated tin pot roof. Others can only begin to wonder what's happening in my lodgings. I don't care. I'm in bliss, in my own little war-torn corner of the world.

Connolly for the third and everything is rosy. I'm sat, relaxed for a change, sipping my way to Sunderland's three points when Wednesday have the audacity to score two in the last ten minutes. Relaxation turns to anxiety, songs turn to expletives and Carlsberg turns to Smirnoff. Fear not though, young foolish one, within a minute new signing Carlos Edwards is on hand to give us comfort and ease at the final whistle. Get in there boys. Still only seventh… actually I can't believe I've said that. Only seventh, we would have settled for top half after Keano took over. Perhaps just a measure of how much life the Irish have pumped back into our club.

Wednesday 24th January 2007

I decided to drive around the outskirts of the camp perimeter security fence to gaze through the wire at the outside world of Afghanistan. It is how I imagined, derelict dried out prairies leading all the way to the distant mountains in the backdrop.

There were a few buildings nearby; the few that were seen were bombed out tower blocks, in which some locals still lived. Outside the kids knocked a football around in bare feet. If we thought we had it bad in life, just look at those children and what they assume is normal life. If being shacked up here with only updates of the Lads is bad enough, being here forever with no radio at all is something even my worst nightmares normally save me from.

Tuesday 30th January 2007

Chipped my tooth and re-opened an old war wound today, which resembles a crucifixion. It occurred by pissing around in the cargo yard, as Jamie the Geordie (of all people) twatted me with a plank of wood, not realising an old rusty Afghan nail was still hammered inside, protruding enough to remain in my hand. It hasn't healed thanks to the fucking dust and the fact the wound is in the crack of my hand, bastards. Not long left now though, as time ticks by slowly. I've never wished my life away so much as my days spent here. I will be past the age of sixty by the time I reach normality, I've wished so much.

On a slow night shift tonight, work is crass, but plentiful enough for me to miss any notification of tonight's results. I wasn't hoping for much against bogey side Palace at our place. I secretly harbour dreams of a scruffy 1-0 win, hopefully going in off that fat, pyjama-wearing tit in goal for the visitors.

I shouldn't be surprised to receive a few raised eyebrows in the internet cabin, some fifteen minute trek away, when I yell "for fuck's sake" through my hoarse cold riddled voice, at the sight of a goalless draw. I'm amazed to be on the computers at all, considering there are around fifteen terminals to cater for over three thousand troops. It is the modern day technological equivalent of Jesus, accompanied by pieces of fish and bread. I find myself rambling once more, trying in vain to forget about the shower of shit I've just read about in the point gained off Palace.

Wednesday 31st January 2007

Work is interfering with my dreams. Last night I dreamt of the match, no one in particular, but instead of having nets in goal, there were aircraft cargo nets chained to the pitch, restricting any passage of play. Work is like some kind of toxic irritant foam bath, armed with a game plan of driving me insane before I depart this godforsaken place. Help me someone, help me please.

The smallest of things are nibbling away at me now, like the sight of seeing naked blokes walking around. I'm sick of seeing an accidental flicker of some geezer's bell end, every time I go for an innocent wee.

FEBRUARY

Saturday 3rd February 2007

Seriously counting down the days now until my departure home. Everything has multiplied considerably though. The mundane feeling, the nuisance of work, the agony of aches and pains, assembled on my four month stretch, the lack of football... I could go on. Can't even be arsed to write, I feel so irritable, tinged with edgy thoughts. A 2-0 win over Coventry winds Scotty – a Sky Blues die-hard – round the bend. I only needed the recently acquired Stern John to score against his old counterparts to really take the piss. Yet another twist and turn in our season, signing Stern John from Coventry, only for him to play against them the very next game, madness.

Sunday 4th February 2007

Our lass informs me that I have an exciting autograph waiting for me, recently obtained at yesterday's match against Coventry. I dream of Gascoigne, Rae or Maldini, not really thinking about what then hell the best defender in Italian history would be doing at the SOL. She reveals it is no less than new Coventry, ex-Sunderland carthorse, Kevin Kyle. Is she winding me up? Answer is no, but it raises a smile anyway. I instruct her to organise folks back home into arranging Quinny's autograph on the matchday programme in future.

Saturday 10th February 2007

Too tired to exist, never mind write. However, great news is offered in the form of a flight booking home to Cyprus on a Hercules aircraft, once more travelling through the Arabian sands of Qatar. I return as I arrived, quite aptly. This basically just meant another vertical take off and climb.

Add to that we beat Plymouth 2-0 and I'm feeling mint inside, just too fatigued to display on the outside. Perhaps cautious optimism is on the agenda, understanding from past events how things can change for the worse, when it comes to military aircraft and delays. Still, we're on a roll now back home, still in seventh, but well in touch with the leaders. New signing from Arsenal Anthony Stokes repays some of his £2m price tag by scoring the opener, with David Connolly wrapping things up.

If things pan out the way I've planned and hoped, then today's Argyle match will be my last match experienced on Afghan soil. Good then to depart on a victory.

Monday 12th February 2007

Tonight has been the scariest moment in my whole time here. Quietly reading the week old newspapers, in our carved out Iso container-cum-crew room, I am sat analysing the reports in the Express about the Falklands conflict, twenty-five years ago this year, when a whistling noise hurtles towards my location, like a steaming kettle about to blow its lid. I ran out to hear the noise was louder, flashing by I could even hear a gust of wind above my position. Five seconds later and the mortar which had just flown a matter of yards above me exploded in the road. I was shocked, but quickly regained my senses, as a second whistling was following suit, heading my way.

It was night and no one could see it coming, making any sort of evasive action almost impossible. It would be literally pot luck where it landed. The whistling screamed by once more, complete with the gust of wind, it was that close, and BANG, a second hit, sending the air raid sirens into full alert.

It was to be the final two mortars of my tour, but the closest I came to kissing my arse goodbye and all within a matter of days until I'm due home. That night shook a few people up. I have never been in a state of shock before, not frantic levels, but a mild dose, where one laughs about the incident, thinking cheeky bastards, having the neck to try and kill me. It's then I remember where I am and that the harshness of the frontline is only over the other side of a mountain.

Monday 19th February 2007

I'm back! Back home in the Mediterranean winter sun of Cyprus. Oh my god, what a journey, what a journey. After being delayed twenty-four hours (told you so) I was finally on my way, minutes before an enormous sandstorm enveloped the Kandahar province.

All day Saturday I couldn't keep still, like an energizer battery on acid, that's wobbly eggs hallucinogen acid, not the usual battery ilk. It was all down to the nerves, combined with excitement. Last time I flew out of here, I was merry on Jack Daniels and whatever I could muster, mainly Dr Pepper or Lemonade. On this occasion I had planned to nip back to the barrack block and retrieve a sly box of red wine I'd stashed, enabling me to guzzle on the contents. Things don't always go to plan, work mainly getting in the way, as people wanted to say their goodbyes and enjoy a chat. I'd be leaving sober as a newt. At least I was out of here, though.

I knew what was coming, what was in store for me. A big fuck off roller coaster in the sky, that wouldn't stop moving until four hours later. The four propeller engines roared, the plane jerked back and we were up flying low level until the end of the runway, turning vertical on completion of the tarmac. Up, down, all around... this is planet Earth. I did ponder to myself, as I had done on my initial arrival in October, "what the fuck am I doing here?" Protected to the max with body armour and helmet, I hung on for dear life, as the Hercules nose-dived, turned on the proverbial sixpence, then shot up further into the clouds. I suppose it didn't help my nerves looking out of the tiny porthole windows the whole time.

After those early teething stages, the remainder of the flight to Qatar settled down, occasionally acting like a speedboat, riding the waves of turbulence, pounding along on our way. Qatar was reached, as my nerves winded down into relaxation mode. First things first on landing, trying to find out the score of Sunderland versus Southend, played at the SOL today. I'd missed the final check on the wireless by a whisker and none of the lads there knew the results.

Once I had gained my bearings and dodged all the Yanks (it's a US airbase remember) I located a small British Forces phone centre.

Our lass spoke straight away...

"Did you hear the score?," this leading me to feel a bout of depression arriving, clearly Sunderland had buggered it up, as she'd never begin a conversation purely based on football. I just want to be home. Hit me with your worst, pet.

"We won 4-0, John scored two, Hysen and Connolly." Bloody quality springs to mind.

"We're in the play-offs now," she added with excited giggles.

Jesus, we'd done it. Sunderland had reached the verge of something good. When I first passed through Qatar in October, we'd struggled to overcome a poor Barnsley side. We then finished the end of play lying in seventeenth position in the league. What a transformation. I could sense it from here, Wearside was awake again, ready to adore their football once more. It's pure brilliance, even from a frustrating long distance.

I slept happy that night, even in my forty-man sweat ridden tent. I could have been flying out to Kandahar again; such were the similarities to the vicinity as last time. The sun was awkwardly bright again, the heat a constant taster of what the desert heat can serve up in the heights of summer. A barren wasteland, sparsely populated, not that I saw much on each visit. Briskly picked up here, hastily dropped off there, complete with instructions for reporting times and point of contact. I'd had enough of this desolated landscape, although beautiful in its own right, it still lacked the lush green rural splendour of England in spring, Cyprus in winter. The news that the final leg of my journey home to the Med might be delayed by a day, or worse still cancelled all together, did not bring joy to my heart on arrival in the office the following day. I'm now tired, in need of a bath, shave and a decent home cooked meal.

I sit back in an office armchair outside and watch the sun go to work on the runway, yards in front of me. My mind is past caring anymore, simply wanting to go home and see my wife, two cats and indulge in a drink or two in the Red and White Tractor. Not to mention enjoying the delights of internet match reports, minus the hassle of waiting in queues, people looking over your shoulder, hurried along throughout the allotted time of half an hour or so.

My lack of focus and anxiety was a result of four months depression, hard graft and constant letdowns. Today though my luck was in. A last minute change of plan meant my flight, albeit five hours late, was back on and scrambled, ready to go within half an hour. One moment I was sat in the same position, daydreaming into the Arabian sunset, the orange beacon, a glowing ember over the darkened sand dunes. The next instance I'm whisked off, as if I were some national celebrity rushed through American checkpoints, arriving in time to go home.

I had always dreamt of the moment when I would return home. It would be a specially chartered aircraft; a big fuck off military band would fanfare my arrival. Niall Quinn himself had jetted over to present my operational medal, as the crowd waved red and white miniature flags in the background. My wife, with the two cats in tow, would run in slow motion, her arms thrust open, planting a huge kiss on my lips, a pint in my hand and a ticket for the next match in the other palm. Then I woke up to reality.

Instead, I was flown in by the backdoor on a sleepy Sunday night, nearly knocking on Monday morning. My ears constantly ringing, as though I had been to a live Prodigy gig, from the repetitive vibration of the four propeller engines. If the miners suffered from vibration white finger, then surely I was inflicted with the white ear version. My flight landed with the minimum of fuss, with an entourage of about four or five people, only there to refuel the aircraft and meet the one passenger – me. No fanfares, no crowds, yet it was one of those moments I'll never forget.

It was akin to scoring in a local derby game with no one to celebrate with, apart from the work colleagues on duty. I can now connect with Michael Gray and perhaps a similar feeling when he grabbed the goal at St. James in 1997, when all away fans were banned. I felt like telling the world I was back, but no one else was awake. Our lass was and Spit who picked me up. A quiet hello, a kiss and I was home. I sat down in the Red and White Tractor and sipped on ice cold Carlsberg, like a 1976 vintage Champagne, reflecting on my thoughts.

Had I just wasted four months of my life in something I didn't believe in? Or had I played my part in something worthwhile, protecting society across the globe from the evils of terror? In any respect it is all political, but we are losing good men. I long for the day when all the troops come home. Here's to life, honour in death and for that superior feeling of celebrating a last minute winner on a Saturday afternoon. We salute you all.

Tuesday 20th February 2007

A day later I feel as though I've been kicked in the bollocks, which in turn have been belted up my windpipe and knocked out my teeth. No it's not the last minute equalizer for Birmingham in our 1-1 draw, in a massive game at St Andrews. And it's not the booze talking, even if I admit to feeling a little punch drunk. I feel empty. What's the point of it all? I'm on a major downer, is this some kind of after-show stress related party? I'm due my debriefing on events out in Afghanistan, but not until six weeks when I'm back at work. I think it will be a long six weeks.

Anyway, Carlos Edwards is on fire and Keano has the matchstick in his hand. Just saw the goal at Brum on Sky's Championship round up. Fucking superb. If we were on a roll before, then we are on a tidal wave now. Up the Premier.

Saturday 24th February 2007

I'm struggling to adapt to normality. I feel empty, no feeling. I should be proud that I've served my country, but I'm not. I haven't achieved anything, as far as I can see. It's a losing battle, in my opinion, not that it counts for much. I'm paid to go where I'm told and lump it in the same breath. I have no problem with that. I signed on the dotted line; I understood what the forces was all about and that's being professional and doing your job to the best of your ability. This still doesn't hide the fact I do not entirely agree with everything I do. No doubt I'll be seeing the delights of Afghanistan in the future. My personal inner negativity is over-come by the positive wave of emotion ravaging Sunderland AFC, at present.

The big games are coming thick and fast now. It was Brum the other day, Der-by County today and West Brom, next Saturday. The top three teams in three games. Our season can be a hit or miss in these such encounters. Football is my saviour, as I practise the regular adopted routine of one's eyes glued to the tele-vision set. Tim and Helen with Soccer AM, a live match and then Soccer Saturday. Whoever thought of the basic, but original concept of positioning ex-footballers commentating on games before a studio camera, whilst every other match is honoured with a live beamback report, was groundbreaking.

It does make for nervous viewing. As well as your team, you keep tabs on the other clubs around you in the league, hearts beating faster whenever a shot is placed at goal, or a raised voice or two.

Today with it being such a high profile game, Sunderland and Derby County fans are provided with an in house studio commentary with Charlie Nicholas, a luxu-ry usually reserved for the Premiership. Every time a mutter, whimper or sneeze was had in the studio, my stomach tensed, heart seized and body stopped. Like playing football poker, the odds and hands dealt each passing minute were becoming increasingly difficult to bear. By now our lass was on the receiving end of my torment, daring not to even look in my direction, as I jumped around like a lunatic on the sofa.

Jeff Stelling: "There's been a penalty at the Stadium of Light, Charlie."

Well it can't be for us I immediately presumed. The last time Sunderland were awarded a spot kick was when Noah was learning to swim at Newcastle Road baths and Ice Age had been produced before Disney was formed.

"It's gone to Sunderland, Jeff."

Fuck me. Oh shit, fucking hell, we've got a penner, shit.

And without time to worry, Connolly, one nil to Sunderland, magic. Being a Sunderland fan, you know not to get carried away, especially in times of fortune, with Nicholas noting the incident as a "soft" decision. Suppose that will make up for all the times we didn't receive one in our favour over the last season and a half. Looks like Mother Teresa couldn't have given away a pen, tough luck, we'll take it.

I hate the scoreline, 1-0. As a fan you can never rest on your laurels, even though without question, you know your team will. Every time we flashed to Charlie for an update, Derby were increasingly on the attack, thus resulting in the inevitable really.

"There's a second goal at the Stadium of Light… but which way has it gone, Charlie," drooled Stelling.

"1-1 Jeff and deservedly so, Giles Barnes for Derby." Bollocks.

Here we go. Our good run is over. The house was silent. The missus and the cats not daring to move, nor look in my direction. I walk out the room and go for a cup of tea, as I now pace the floor. The tea transforms into a can of lager to ease my palpitations, now attacking my chest in an influx of waves.

Time ticks on into the last ten minutes of the match. A goal now would secure three points for either side.

"Come on Sunderland," I mildly spit through gritted teeth. I muster all my will power to the god of fate, reminding him of all the wretched luck we as Sunderland have crawled through over the years. I always resort to this as a last ditch tactic, pleading with the football heavens to inspire our fortunes from somewhere deep down. It never works.

The final scores begin to bombard the screen, as a flurry of red highlights all the games which have reached their conclusion. Sunderland and Derby remain in white, meaning they're still playing. And then the ultimately terrifying words are spoken. A gasp and a pause from Jeff Stelling. He breaks away from the onrushing full times, to exclusively reveal, a development, almost in slow motion.

"And there has been a third goal at the Stadium of Light... this could be absolutely crucial to the run-in of the Championship, but who has got it?"

My head was now thrust into my hands, fingers allowing my eyes to peak through the gaps, if I dared.

"Just fucking tell us yer bastards," eager to be put out of my misery, as I envisage Sunderland 1 Derby 2 to flash up underneath Charlie Nicholas' face.

"It's Liam Miller, Jeff, 2-1 to Sunderland," enthused the TV pundit.

I go to scream, but no sound comes out. My voice box is refusing to exact orders from my brain, which in fairness could be sending out all sorts of signals, as my internal system crashes like a laptop in water.

The missus cheers for me, as we look at each other in delight. My recovery is quick; I leap around akin to a child who's just played a practical joke on their teacher.

"Come on Sunderland, come on, come on, come on," I mutter out loud, desperate for the three peeps of the final whistle. I conclude that watching the game in this manner, through the power of television, is more stressful than attending the match. At least the fans present can witness first hand a goal scored or conceded. With the digital media on satellite channels, the outcome is a game of chance, for those daring to take it on the chin.

Jeff Stelling: "And it's all over at the Stadium of Light."
"Yeeeeeeeeesssssssss!," echoes off the four sitting room walls.

My feelings of triumph are matched by the scenes shown on the screen, as players and fans celebrate as one.

"Fucking Liam Miller, you beauty," as I punch the air, jubilant now for the remainder of the weekend. Imagine if football were related to narcotic drugs. They'd be dealing ecstasy pills called Last Minute Winners or Liam Millers, instead of White Doves or Christmas Trees.

"Got any Liam Millers mate?" would come the cry inside the Blue Monkey, if it were still open.

You don't need drugs to support Sunderland. Come to think of it, of course you do. It's enough to send you over the edge. No wonder I've got grey hair. Like a big kid I need to hear the classified scores, the excellence of listening to the Sunderland score again. And like a big kid, one has to perform a wah hey after the score has been read out. Class.

MARCH

Saturday 3rd March 2007

The days are flying past now. After wishing so many of my days away in Kandahar, I'm now trying in vain to reverse the trend. If I could physically put the clocks back I would, as my leave whittles down to a number of weeks.

Still, it's Saturday, which means another day of frenzy, another ninety minutes of fear, with Sunderland playing third place West Brom at The Hawthorns. That means second, top and third place teams in just twelve days. Keano said it would be make or break and at the moment it's make. I'm only waiting for it to break, as any weathered Sunderland follower can only look forward to at some point in their continuous heartache supporting the lads.

Oh Ye of little faith.

John Salako was Sky TV's choice of reporter this time, cramped into one corner of the Albion ground, just enough to capture the shenanigans of the away contingent of travelling red and white. And it was this section of the ground celebrating first, with me quivering in me pants, to no avail, with Dwight Yorke opening the scoring. Surely our bubble must burst sooner or later, but no, Stern John pops up to make it two goals to the good. I was in football heaven. Everything we do at the moment is coming off. I now wish it was the end of the season. Well maybe not, what I mean is I wish for us to end the season in this manner. After all, I think I have wished away enough of my life this year.

Ex-Mackem Darren Carter makes it 2-1, but I feel a lot calmer, confident throughout the final stages of the match. What the hell is going on? Me a seasoned Sunderland fan, calming down, feeling natural restraint, when watching the results flow in like high tide. Perhaps it's my stress related war illness, which has not been fully exposed yet. I can't wait until I go full blown, I'll be cheering on the opposition, or something completely insane.

Some argue that football is a game based on superstition. There are many of us who adopt this principle, whether it be in the dressing room, a routine on the way to the match, or the pub in which we drink in. For today's encounter with the Baggies, I decided to inspire the lads on by copying my same routine as the last time we played Albion this season, on a sweltering Bank Holiday Monday, back in August. On that occasion, my friends, wife and I enjoyed a summer barbecue, as Quinny's last match as manager heralded a positive new dawn in Sunderland's season. And so despite the early cross winds of March blowing up yonder in our back garden, another barbecue was had, to aid the lads to victory, for a second consecutive time, as we chomp on our chops, al fresco style.

The only thing that riled me that day was the lack of acknowledgment by Roy Keane in his after match interviews to our collective contribution, swinging the result in favour of the Black Cats by placating the footballing gods of fate with a spring barbecue. Not one thank you to the Cyprus supporters branch from Keano. You'd think the players and the gaffer had done it all by themselves, or something. I'm prepared to let this one go, this one time only.

Perhaps, the football TV channels should concentrate their build up to a match through the eyes of a fan, instead of talking the same old bollocks, to the same old individuals, quoting freely sickening football punch lines, such as "it's a game of two halves" or "the next goal will be the most important." Instead, pick any fan to tell it like it is, show archive footage of a fan's match day routine, the last time these two particular sides played and if the routine would be continued today. I'd rather watch fat Stan's pre-pub banter, than Garth Crooks orally ovulating over some retired cockney wide boy, posing questions over half an hour long. Is this a valid point of constructive criticism, has war made me bitter, or have the immaculate standards of Keano rubbed off on my footballing world? All will be revealed, in next week's episode…

Thursday 8th March 2007

Last night I experienced a monumental fantasy, dreamt with mirage propor-tions. It was linked back to my time away. I'd returned captured by my own peo-ple, charged with war crimes. I pleaded my innocence, but to no avail. I was to be sentenced to my punishment, but first I would face my trial and this was the strange part.

I was marched towards the front of the baying crowd, flanked by two armed es-corts. Step by step, we marched ever closer, as I carried an axe, with which I was to be dealt with. It was a march not of military standard, veering more towards Monty Python's funny walks, but all taken in serious context nevertheless.

I glanced over to look at my two surrounding escorts to notice they were not human, but in fact creatures of feline features. In fact they were house cats… my house cats. I looked over to Samson, of the grey tabby variety, to which he gave a cheeky nod of the head and wink, swinging his arms, still carrying his rifle. It was as if to say "You're in the shit now mate."

With that I woke up to find both cats, now back to household size, lying either side, minus the weapons. And in a twist of fate, Samson raised his head to see what all the commotion was about.

What is happening to me? I'm a nervous wreck. But is that through combat stress or supporting Sunderland? I would hazard a guess at the latter.

Saturday 10th March 2007

Barnsley away today, meaning a slight change to the Cyprus crackpot, après-war, matchday schedule.

Some things never change in England, but by the sounds of things, they are reverting back to the dark ages of pre-Hillsborough. The subject in question, the Neanderthal treatment of away fans by the steward mafia, but more incredibly by various police forces around the country.

And so onto Barnsley today. A staggering eight thousand travelling fans are on the road to support their team, at probably one of the closest away games of the season in South Yorkshire. However, this region's police force (or farce?) stick their oar in, bring the kick off time forward to 1.30pm and proceed to ban all alcohol on sale in the ground for the said Mackem hordes.

In today's preposterous world of political correctness is this nothing short of prejudice in all its glory? How the hell can they get away with treating football fans as second-class citizens? For years now a minority of police constabularies have continued the animal herding tactics of shepherding fans into the pen of the ground, then holding them back after a game, without question. More frightening now though, is that more regional forces have jumped on the Stone Age bandwagon of shitting on the away following, for daring to ruin their weekends off.

For instance, take my brother-in-law's story. He booked his train journey down to Barnsley in order to arrive with ample time to sample a few friendly drinks in the area, then amble to the ground, perhaps a swift pint inside, then watch his football team in peace. However, because of the new improvised kick off time, he now had under half an hour to dash to the ground from the railway station, where on arrival no alcohol was to be consumed. This could have led to a building level of frustration, which in some cases could cause angry flashpoints, as the police ruin everyone's day out. As a result of the coppers' wisdom, this group of lads, whom to be fair enjoy a social drink at the game (and why not, after they've been to work all week to pay for their day out) resorted to binge drinking on the train, to reach optimum levels of jovial spirits, which may have been construed as illegal public order disturbances.

Our club wanted more than the eight thousand tickets given, in a bid to eclipse the legendary 1991 trip to Maine Road, then home of Manchester City, where the marker was set for all supposed big clubs with a die hard following, with over fifteen thousand Mackems cheering on the Lads. On police advice Barnsley turned down Sunderland's overtures of extra income, even though their own sections of Oakwell were nowhere near capacity. If the police here can't handle such a huge number of people in one place, I recommend none of them transfer to London's Metropolitan branch, where protests and their ilk are dished out on a near daily basis.

In the end, the team provided the perfect day out overcoming Barnsley 2-0, with Grant Leadbitter and a last minute David Connolly belter our reward.

For me it was less enthralling. Having endured a Mongolian sized hangover, I rolled around on my alcohol-induced sickbed, barely able to press the buttons on the TV remote control. After a concoction of pain killers (dissolvable to reach the bloodstream fast), comfort food in the form of tomato soup and lashings of sugary English tea, I found myself well enough to mildly celebrate at the end of play. Another classic result; come on lads, unbeaten until the end of the season, why not?

How I longed to be part of the red and white revolution, to be part of the travelling masses. In fact to be at any football match would suffice.

Back in Afghanistan, I had dreamed of the day I would see live football again. I had meticulously planned potential games in my head, ready for the planning of exhausted travel arrangements ahead. I'd maybe spend some time with my wife, relax in Cyprus, see the sights, visit the beach, but then thoughts would focus on the possibilities of flying home for a game. I had already been placed on a course back in the UK, to take place in April, maybe allowing me to catch the Colchester away game afterwards. Or perhaps add more leave on, to witness my first home game of the season, with Hull pencilled in as the main date. Flights had been examined, rail journeys analysed, away tickets searched, in hope of my imminent return. Akin to a long drawn out boardroom takeover saga, my frustration of arranging the complete package to visit home shores and pay homage to my personal religion of football was now reaching boiling point.

Monday 12th March 2007

I look forward to tomorrow. A day embedded deep into the middle of my six week leave, not a care in the world, well not quite, but for tomorrow, they're all discarded. All eyes are on Sunderland, live on Sky, live in my front room, no distractions, plenty of alcohol, good grub, pure quality.

I just hope I'm not too drunk before the match at home to Stoke. I can't help it in a way, as I know the nerves will be eating away at my insides. I'm desperate for a win, desperate for a performance, desperate for a deafening atmosphere to show off to the watching world.

Tuesday 13th March 2007

In all probability – written prior to Stoke City

I hereby write this on Tuesday the 13th of March 2007. I enclose my predictions for the remainder of the season, in order to prove how much I think I know my club – Sunderland AFC.

Tonight's game against Stoke could be a classic case of Sunderland messing things up in one of the easier matches they've recently had. We always tend to do things the hard way, normally resulting in the lads winning at the big boys' grounds when the pressure's on, then lapsing into a world of self congratulations by pulling off a piss poor performance. And tonight's game is a classic scenario, with the added bonus of Sunderland playing live on TV. This brings the added attraction of potential extra fans, which surely merits a bland red and white performance every time. However, I believe in the presence of Keano and the winning mentality the fella brings with him. Combine this with my positive head on and I'll plum for a home win, albeit very marginal.

From there we soldier on to another home game against strugglers Hull City. Had it been at the KC Stadium, then perhaps I would have swung in favour of The Tigers. Again I envisage a narrow SOL victory for the lads, maybe 1-0, or 2-1. Cardiff away will end in defeat. My Red and White heart is struggling to cope with the immense pressure and expectation, which sees the players succumbing to their first defeat of the season at Ninian Park. Cardiff will present a tough battle and they've already beaten us at the SOL. Put ex-Mag Chopra up front and he's bound to score, meaning we are fighting a losing battle, I reckon he'll get a goal, which will be enough to win it.

A crunch match bigger than our Welsh encounter arrives on April 7th, when old foes Keano and McCarthy come to blows. A cracking match with superb atmosphere will finish with a last minute winner, probably from a set play, step up Jonny Evans.

The last of the tricky games and Southampton away. Burley's men take the lead, with the lads pouncing in the last ten minutes for a draw. QPR at home up next on the menu and a resounding 3-0 home win, so I reckon, then a 2-1 victory at Colchester and despite Stevie Caldwell providing a potential spanner in the works, Sunderland should overcome a faded Burnley and progress 2-0.

The final game does have its concerns though. Luton are scrapping for survival now, nevermind come May and being at home it could be nervy. A 1-0 win to settle it either way.

Throughout it all though, I have a sneaky feeling that Sunderland will be promoted automatically, behind Birmingham, thanks to Roy Keane's never say die attitude, now instilled into our ever bonding team. Yet knowing Sunderland as I do, it will go down to the last kick of the ball before there is any celebration for the Wearside faithful.

Whatever happens, we are forever in debt to Messrs Quinn and Keane for turning our club around. I mean just look at Leeds.

Après Stoke

Sunderland never fail to disappoint. A lacklustre 2-2 draw on a night when fortunately other results went in our favour, was total bollocks. I promised myself I would not become irritated, but after that, how could I not? We were awful, living up to our typical stage fright TV antics.

I scared the cats and the missus, as she took heed of the neighbour's needs. "Fuck them" I raged, turned and ranted more at the TV. The two bottles of wine and Guinness didn't help matters. I nearly resorted to phoning my mate Spit and have him come round with fifteen minutes left. A kind of fans' super sub. He'd always been there when Sunderland performed well on the box. And I'd always been there when Spurs (his team) had buggered things up big style. So in retrospect he should have made an appearance for us.

As it happens things could have been worse. But then that's always the case supporting Sunderland. Had we won, we'd have pissed on the rest of the league, who had equally mucked things up tonight. Only Preston won out of the top ten. Mind you, I'd have settled for a point off the Stoke match, especially Daryl Murphy scoring in the last minute. Pity the wife didn't see it like me. I will have to calm down if I'm to see this season out still in wedded bliss.

Wednesday 14th March 2007 – The day after Stoke

I have a sore throat from inevitably sleeping with my mouth open and abusing the TV screen last night. It feels like Samson the cat has poured half of his litter tray down my gob and judging by the smell of my breath, with all the shit in it too.

Now we have finally had broadband internet connected, a big thing in a technological sense in Cyprus, I've visited the web a few times, glancing at a few quotes. Taking last night's result into perspective, I conclude it's not a bad result. It will hopefully continue to stimulate the players' mindsets, whilst whetting their appetite to perform better on Saturday against Hull.

Again, it's frustrating to see Sunderland blow a great opportunity of gaining ground on the top two, Derby and Birmingham. Hopefully the TV cameras will disperse for the remainder of the season, obviously bar Southampton away.

I should really learn to control myself and think of the neighbours. I'm sure they didn't appreciate the expletives thrown at the TV towards midnight, earlier this morning. Maybe it's my stress syndrome kicking in. The missus doesn't look at me on a match day, poor lass. I promise to keep calm on Saturday, provided we are 3-0 up in the first ten minutes.

Friday 16th March 2007 Pre- Hull

Man flu has arrived in surround sound, detailing me to bed for three days now, applying more misery to my newfound manic depression. It's St Patrick's Day tomorrow as well, coupled with the Hull game and I might be in bed for both – the second Saturday running laden with illness. However, it worked last week at Barnsley, so I'm willing to take another hit for the team.

I've thought about mixing some fizzy paracetamols with some Famous Grouse, which I have found in the vaults of the Red and White Tractor, à la scene in the Brit flick Layer Cake. Instead, I've opted to pour the Grouse into an instant mocha coffee to see if the effect can numb the pain in my sinuses. All this and I should have been at the SOL tomorrow, if all the flights went to plan, bastards. I could do with a stroke of good luck. The way I'm feeling, though, I sense it's only a stroke headed my way.

Our lass tried to cheer me up by standing over me, akin to a bunny boiler, whilst in the bath. This was in a bid to frighten the shit out of me on opening my eyes and popping my head from under the water, after washing my hair. Needless to say, I nearly shat myself, leaving her in hysterics in a routine to propel me on Soccer AM's MMS alert section, where scaring random folk has been the order of the day most recently. With me being ill, I didn't see the funny side of things. However, I took revenge by pissing in the bath water she was about to embrace. That'll learn yer!

Anyhow, I'll get back to my pit and recuperate, getting up once again to watch Southampton versus Colchester on the box tonight. A goalless draw will suffice, keeping both teams at bay from the play-off zone. If I had my way, I'd keep the rest of the league at bay from the play-off zone too.

I was planning to nip into work today to sort out my leave for the crucial month of May. The cold from hell put paid to that. I'll try again tomorrow. It's a priority as I require Luton away off, as well as covering all of the potential play-off games. A phone call from Spit at work reveals I'm on a course at the beginning of June and

I will find it easier to put leave either side of it, meaning time off for the Wembley bound final. The course though is still not confirmed, just like all other aspects of my life. Where's that Grouse?

Saturday 17th March 2007 – St. Patrick's Day

I decided to have a two-for-one special offer in the Red and White Tractor to celebrate the Irish saint. I've ended up with a Celtic pick 'n' mix of Magners cider, Guinness and Caffrey's.

Obviously after getting stuck into that selection of booze, Soccer Saturday flew by and I was somewhat calm, too calm for my liking. Sunderland eased to a 2-0 victory, with goals at either end of the game. Jonny Evans and Stern John were the providers of joy.

It's now past midnight and my jovial upbeat mood has dispersed to give way to negative thoughts about my crumbling plans to witness a Sunderland game first hand.

I delayed phoning my sister, mainly on the subject of acquiring Luton tickets. Whilst everything is set up in place, our lass is somewhat cautious about it. Well that would be an understatement. In fact she is adamant "I'm not setting foot on a flight to Luton for two days to see a friggin' football match." There is no hiding from the fact that it will cost over £300 for the weekend in Bedfordshire. Throw into the equation the element of disappointment after the lack of enthusiasm from some of the lads back home, on wanting tickets for the said match. It's OK for them; they can watch a match anytime. I'm doing me nut, sat here thousands of miles away, watching all the drama unfold. Then there is the chance that Sunderland will enter the play-offs, meaning further travel arrangements in May. Yet if I delay my proposed flight any longer, then prices may rise, as people fill the airline's seats.

What do I do, what do I do, what do I do? Add a few doses of depression to flavour and I've a real miserable concoction bubbling in my head. I've decided to grow a beard until I return to work (in two weeks) to take my mind off it all. I now look like Gattuso of AC Milan. I'll be back in the UK soon anyway, when I'm sectioned for turning insane. It's not the football, I don't know what it is, but I can't sleep, I talk to myself, feel empty inside, lonely on the outside, with no particular interest to socialise with people. The more I think about this condition, the more I worry. This is not normal. Yet I think people would take the piss if I owned up to being demoralised, depressed, as I wasn't exactly a frontline soldier. Maybe, I've become accustomed to fighting a losing battle for four months, it has now become ingrained into my system, akin somewhat to Sunderland AFC and its own rotting losing mentality when Niall Quinn took over. Then there is the issue that all the other lads in my section have returned home from Afghanistan seemingly normal, or at least that is how they appear on the outside. I'm afraid that I have been in a staple routine of feeling down, that I don't know how to smile or enjoy life anymore.

Would a return home to the UK help matters? Go and see my bonny Sunderland, to lift my sprits, take my mind elsewhere. Heavy stuff to be buzzing round my head. Too heavy for St Patrick's Day, and it's not the drink, all my pondering that has made the effects of alcohol wear off.

At least there was a decent crowd at the match today, over thirty eight thousand in fact. Reports from back home suggest that flights from the Republic of Ireland to Ponteland Airport are at a premium on Sunderland match days, with extra charters on for today's game. Long may it continue, as we welcome new fans to the addictive drug of supporting Sunderland AFC. Poor bastards, very much like The Matrix – just take the blue tablet and you will wake up in Dublin or Cork, none the wiser. Dare to swallow the red and white pill and you will awake to reality, ten years later, suffering with a drink problem, a comedown of adrenalin and an unhealthy portion of hope still beating in your heart… all from a hop across the Irish Sea to see the heroes in red and white.

Speaking of tablets, I'll have to down a sleeping variety, or I will be awake all night, even though my eyes are burning through lack of moisture present around the pupil. Sweet dreams…

…It's 2am local time in Cyprus. I've had too much Chilean red merlot for my liking, but enough to ease the pressures of my sinuses… for now.

After randomly searching on the internet, I've come up with a few scorching ideas. Initially looking for bar accessories for the Red and White Tractor, I indulged into one of those magical mystery tours in cyberspace, eyeing up a whole new world of miscellaneous products that can land you in trouble, especially sat at the computer table pissed.

For example, bar accessories lead to fancy dress, which then twists into the topic of Star Wars head masks. The mad idea then moved in my brain to ordering an executive box for the Luton game in May, wear suits and a Star Wars character mask, purely for comedy value and rich banter. My plan then evolved into obtaining a retro inflatable each to spur on the innocent antics of the day. This event would be solely based on us appearing in some kind of business section for the day. After another brief glance at the Luton Town official website, cheekily noticed by chance, was the fact that tickets were now eventually on sale for the home section for the Sunderland game. Fucking hallelujah. For weeks I've constantly checked the Hatters' home page, like a mother goose checking her eggs.

And with that, Operation Cuckoo will be put into floatation, as a group of us will enter the Luton Town nest, in order to create our own supporting vicinity to cheer on the Lads to promotion. Clever or what? My sister shall be phoned as soon as I wake up, with the message of phoning Luton and ordering tickets before every other Mackem catches on. We require her services due to the proximity of her safe Essex billing address.

I've noticed a new routing on Monarch's website, advertising flights from Larnaca to London Luton, either side of the final weekend. Pure class. I'll jump on a plane, hang around Luton, celebrate promotion and catch the return flight. All I need now is confirmation. I'll have the leave confirmed; only authorisation is required from Air Force One (our lass) to give me the green light to book away. Too good to be true?

Sunday 18th March 2007

Our lass finally cracked today. Firstly at me for watching Goals on Sunday, followed by three live games, coupled with flicking through channels, quietly observing the football events in Scotland. Second and by no means last, she snapped at the fact my depressed state is driving her crazy. Cue a heart to heart and the revelation that she has found some decent flights in order for me to watch the Luton game. All I need to do is confront work, sort out leave and have my sister ring Luton. There is bound to be some kind of obstacle in the way, but here's hoping.

I still fancy the boys to claim automatic promotion, even though Birmingham acquired a draw at West Brom today. Neither side looked like promotion material to me. Hopefully Brum's luck will end soon.

Little does our lass realise that if things go wrong at Kenilworth Road, I'll be needing a return flight to the UK, to cheer the lads through the play-offs and a visit to the new Wembley. I'll even go AWOL, if needs be. Afghanistan or promotion – there's not much contest, really.

Monday 19th March 2007

Today if ever, completely sums up my luck, feelings and possibly the make up of Sunderland's season. The joyous breakthrough of locating flights from Cyprus to the North East, which were less than a million pounds, was then backed up with swift negotiations at work, where sufficient confirmed leave was obtained. The final cog in the wheel being the securing of the priceless match tickets, hastily settling for anywhere inside Kenilworth Road.

Please be upstanding then, Luton Town Football Club, for ruining my day – the wankers. My new senior translator under the guise of Operation Cuckoo was my sister Helen, who was under firm instructions to order tickets anywhere. If asked, or prompted, the story would go that she is buying them for her brother, a staunch Hatter, who would be celebrating his 30th birthday at the game in question. Considering they were now on general sale, what could go wrong?

Within two or three minutes there was a phone call reply. I initially thought I'd handed out the incorrect number.

"They said they couldn't give me any tickets as I'm not registered on their database for this season."

Fucking bollocks. A fucking disgrace.

How hard is it to buy football tickets these days? You'd assume a club like Luton would need all the guaranteed income they can muster, considering their current predicament. I was fucking fuming. All my plans, once again, turned to rat shit. In a vain attempt to pursue new avenues, though mainly clutching at straws, I e-mail contacts back on Wearside, as well as researching various Luton fan websites. From there I e-mail a number of Town associates, with an obvious cock and bull story to boot.

My initial thoughts were of anger, hoping that small clubs like these twats go down, as they don't deserve to cater for the bigger leagues if they can't handle selling routine tickets. And by the way, get a bigger ground.

Now I've calmed down, exchanged heated words with our lass and then apologised, she has pointed out that it was not meant to be. She indicated that every time I have tried to arrange something this season, barriers have obstructed me in every sense.

In that train of thought then, I have decided that enough is enough. Luton will have to slide, whilst Sunderland will have to aim for the play-offs, if only for my selfish goal of attending at least one Sunderland match this campaign. Perhaps a visit to Wembley is my destiny. Our lass reckons in her wisdom that something somewhere is advising me not to travel, as only bad things will happen. Cheers Angie.

I just don't know. I feel I'm fighting a losing battle trying to watch my beloved red and whites. Yet I will not let the bastards grind me down. My plans are to be re-hacked. The Luton leave will be cancelled tomorrow, with new fresh leave reserved for the play-off final. The biggest gamble of my supporting career… we'll soon see.

On a lighter note, I was informed over the phone from my dad that I had an article in Sunderland's matchday programme from Saturday's game against Hull City. He pointed out my comments that I lied about returning home for the game. This brought a wry smile to my face. It was my initial intention to be present at the match, but fate decided against it. Little did I think it would happen again to me today.

Wembley, Wembley, we're the greatest football team and we're going to Wembley.

Wednesday 21st March 2007

Fate has decreed a twist on my fortunes of obtaining a ticket for the Luton Town away game. After slumping into a childish sulk and tantrum, I composed myself, considered my thoughts and researched a little on the internet. From there I e-mail new Luton contacts, including fanzines and their ilk. I did this yesterday, with only one reply received today. It was to be honest, one more than I had expected. In the e-mail, the lad stated that he has forwarded on my spoof story to the Luton Town club secretary. Shit! What have I started now? I was soon calmed by the fact that from my own personal dealings with football clubs in the past, nothing positive ever came of the situation anyway. However, on checking my inbox later today, I found a response from who else, but the club secretary.

In her reply, she stated that she would be "delighted" to hear from me, adding they would also be prepared to display a birthday message on the Kenilworth scoreboard, coupled with an audio message over the tannoy system, thus relaying my bull shit story to all and sundry, present at the match. Bollocks! What have I done? My sister is on standby again, but what did I write to the geezer in the first place? Luckily, he had replied to my e-mail, with my original plea in tow.

Well then… apparently it is my sister's surprise 40th birthday present. Paranoia takes hold. It is not going to be the routine ramblings of a standard ticket purchase. The club secretary will ask questions and the like. I had better concoct a story in advance to cover all bases and scenarios.

I have already mentioned the fact that none of our family live in Luton, as we all live abroad, or in Scotland. I check a map of the Bedfordshire area, in order to pass on local information, when asked what part of the region our family originally derives from. By chance, the search engine on the web displays results of more than one area entitled Luton. There is also a Luton in Devon and another in Medway, Kent. Ah ha…a plan is forming. I will inform my covert operations officer-cum-sister to pass on in her undercover guise that our other sister supports Luton Town, as this was the name of our village in Devon, just outside Exeter, where we resided until living abroad. I should be a novelist. Hopefully, she will go for that, as I try in vain not to let this lie get out of hand. Knowing my luck, the secretary will have long lost relatives in the South West. I only need to persuade my sister to enact this spaghetti junction of bollocks and verbal mayhem over the phone. Here goes…

…I can now confirm that Operation Cuckoo is now back in full force and in optimum surround sound stereo mode. After delicately phoning my sister (call sign Mother Goose) in Essex, she replied with a phone call some fifteen minutes later to reveal that I owe her £71, for four tickets to Luton. Get in there lass!

"What a fraud I feel," she claimed, tinged with a slight hint of laughter.

Our sis went on to note that the basis we were turned away in the first instance was purely down to security issues and the fact that Sunderland AFC had asked for a staggering 8,000 tickets. Good on them. Once again the new SAFC quietly dispelling the inept attitude towards fans, shown by the previous regime. It was then pointed out that Luton Town shouldn't overlook their own supporters with special circumstances as ours, yet they had to take a hard stance on this, being such a high profile game, with every Sunderland fan and their dog trying to attend. At least the Hatters had done their homework on our loyal support. A pity for them then that they could not see through our patter.

All that was left to complete the deal was the wording for the half time birthday announcement and scoreboard message. Ha, I admit I pissed my pants all day in hysterics just at the thought of it. My other sister (call sign Birthday Girl) would be celebrating her 40th birthday four years and three days early in front of thousands of travelling Mackems, who may know her husband. In the end, the Luton (Devon) story was not required, as Mother Goose blagged her way to legendary status. In fact both sisters played their part, both voluntary and involuntary, respectively.

My dad was first in the queue for the newly claimed 'home' tickets and the brother-in-law only happy to use them, should he not be invited by SAFC to purchase tickets for the away end. Not to mention then that my mate Ged was over the moon that I'd rung him out of the blue with the offer of a ticket, whilst other pal Nick had his reservations about jaunting around home territory, after past expeditions had gone haywire. Everyone I spoke to could not believe the lengths I had slumped to in acquiring the gold dust tickets, but I would think most Mackems would do the same to see their team. Hopefully, all of us can keep our composure and manage to stay inside the ground until the end, when the Championship trophy is held aloft.

Mother Goose is slightly concerned about the fact we might get caught. I told her not to worry, as she'd only be blacklisted by Luton and considering she doesn't even like football, then she has nothing to worry about. I still can't believe it myself. After all the agony, upset and heartache trying to attend a game, it looks like I have succeeded at the final whistle. I know only too well that circumstances can change rapidly and so I'm not counting my air miles yet.

I take back what I said about Luton and their deserved relegation. I do find it intriguing how most football clubs realise that most Sunderland fans would sell their own grandmother to witness a Black Cats match. In a way I take the whole saga as an element of respect for the size of our club in making it difficult to purchase tickets. It has now become a way of life, part of the fun, part of the challenge of following Sunderland Association Football Club on the road.

Operation Cuckoo has beamed out as an initial success. All I need to do now is to coax the lads into wearing fancy dress for a laugh. Maybe those Star Wars masks could get an airing after all. Mine will arrive shortly, with my choice of character – Greedo the alien bounty hunter. All purely for banter of course. I can't see the old man going for the idea, but at least it would hide the fact that Birthday Girl will not be present at the ground.

Thursday 22nd March 2007 a.m.

I was rather inebriated last night, too much for my own good in celebration of my Cuckoo exploits, and so like a twat I e-mail You're on Sky Sports, the live football TV phone in show. The reason being that the studio guest for the night is former Sunderland forward, Don Goodman. I ask him who were the greatest fans he played before and does he recall the Big Bad Don t-shirts doing the rounds at Roker Park in the early nineties, courtesy of fanzine ALS.

I only realised afterwards that if any Luton Town fans were watching, they would no doubt recognise my name and in return contact the club, surely banning my trip home before it had begun. What a tit. Maybe a touch of nervous paranoia, but still something that may jeopardise the journey.

At least Don answered with grace, admitting his son still wears the fans' adulation t-shirt to bed. Ha ha, fair play mate.

As my brain strolls down Paranoid Road, I googled myself to see if any Luton spies could track my Wearside prejudice. To my horror, a list of articles appears, for various publications, with my name connected. I'm in the shit if they check.

Thursday 22nd March 2007 p.m.

It's now the afternoon of the day after the eventful proceedings of yesterday. I'm drained through all the emotion and bottles of plonk sporadically placed around the house. Operation Cuckoo still seems to be in full swing, even after my blunder live on Sky Sports. I have also remembered that I e-mailed fellow Sky Sports show Soccer AM with a photo of me and the lads serving out in Kandahar. Jokingly I commented that all participants on the photo were Sunderland fans, obviously winding up the Boro, Dundee United and Reading fans in the picture. This again may backfire if any Luton associate is watching. I also went one further and sent in an extreme cold weather face mask, which are issued to serving members of the Armed Forces. This was in a bid to receive a Heroes t-shirt that the TV show returns as a gift. At least I never mentioned Sunderland in the letter accompanying the mask.

All that commotion yesterday, I even shat myself laughing so hard on the phone. As I say, eventful all round.

Alas the tickets have already arrived at Mother Goose's house. What a result. She is still worried as the tickets all have her name printed on the front retained portion. I've told her not to worry, as it will only be for the club's records, as she would be the one attending court proceedings if it all kicks off. That had her biting like a bugger. It's too easy.

Friday 23rd March 2007

I received last Saturday's home programme against Hull today, along with the previous midweek publication versus Stoke. It's another factor of living away from the North East, small things like reading the programme a week late. When the brown envelope does arrive though, it's magic. You can lose yourself for a good half hour on the bog and pretend you're in the Blue Bell or Flying Boat, sharing the banter and stats of that day's game.

I'd written an article that appeared in the Hull edition. It was based on my time in Afghanistan and my planned journey to go and watch the lads at the Tigers' game. I also noted that I had pencilled in Colchester away, thanks to a works course being held near the Essex area. Another fact of life is that things change quickly in the Forces, as circumstances saw me shelve both games. Now I look like an idiot in the programme of all places. I wonder if the lads back home read it and thought I was ignoring them. Better go and text them to put the record straight.

I have also cancelled plans to watch Cyprus entertain Slovakia at Nicosia tomorrow. I had initially told Spit that the home side were facing the Czech Republic in a bid to persuade him along. This duly went wrong on hearing that it was in fact the Czech's less glamorous neighbours, Slovakia, playing after all. Never mind, this tactic had worked before in the random rogue sporting event that is the Cyprus International Football Tournament. I had told the lads the Cypriots were playing Holland in a friendly, when all along I knew it was Greece versus Belarus instead. A tactic deployed because none of the lads were as barmy as me to sit there and watch quirky indiscriminate international teams, like me. Needless to say, they were not amused on entering the ground. At least they were the current European Champions, I argued. And so not that fortunate this time, although it will allow me to take in the England Under 21 game at the new Wembley and a break from the norm of persistent worrying engaged during a term of Soccer Saturday. Perhaps that programme is akin to a phobia, perhaps like a fear of flying. After all, you aren't in control in either situation.

I suppose every cloud has a silver lining, every own goal a piece of history.

Saturday 24th March 2007

I'm chomping at the bit to see the finale of Sunderland's Championship campaign continue to romp in. Therefore, I'm disappointed by the international break up of club fixtures. A healthy diet of England U21s followed by Ireland against Wales is hampered by the appearance of the England first team clowning around in Israel.

I admit I hate watching England. The constant drone of watching overrated prima donnas, played out of position by a yes man in charge sends me into apathy. Add that to hearing the old boys network of Hoddle and Redknapp, verbally wanking over their colleagues on the pitch, makes me physically sick. Send in the likes of Allardyce, Paul Jewell and Mike Newell, who tell it like it is. McClaren clearly out of his depth merely keeps up the mundane standards inherited from the equally clueless Sven.

We are rubbish at present. England as a nation expects, and every time the team fail to deliver. I sincerely hope England draw with Andorra (although highly unlikely) meaning we can then oust the plonker in charge.

Fuck Lampard off, play Gerrard in the middle, Lennon on the right and keep the "likely lads" of Rooney, Ferdinand et al on their toes. Substitute them if they are not performing, as was Rooney tonight. That is half of the trouble, they all expect a game, and thus resulting in the bollocks we watch on every occasion.

Get Nosworthy and Leadbitter in there. They can't do any worse than those gets, obsessed with passing sideways and pass and move, just without the move bit. It's no good if you can't keep possession. Pity Beckham wasn't playing.

Sunday 25th March 2007

As it transpired, the decision not to attend the Cyprus/Slovakia match proved to be a correct one. With the money paid out for flights home in May and a payment for Luton tickets, minus the usual monthly debits, we've no money left in the bank until payday on Friday. This hasn't amused our lass one bit. I'm currently raiding the penny jar, or rather Cyprus cents jar. We are even using caster sugar, found in the lofts of the kitchen cupboards, to substitute for the regular granulated sugar in mugs of tea, as we have run out.

Yet I have faith in my football club, as it will all be worth the battle of obtaining tickets, organizing our itinerary and controlling our mid-marriage arguments.

Come May, I hope to be celebrating with champagne, to erase all memories of drinking bloody caster sugar, normally reserved for baking. One thing is for sure, Keano's cooking up a treat for our beloved team.

Tuesday 27th March 2007

I read on the on the SAFC website today that the Luton away game at the end of the season is by invitation only for Sunderland fans. Thus meaning only fans with enough loyalty points accumulated over the years can attend. Cue a mad rush towards the Luton ticket office by Mackems all over the world. I must admit I feel a tingle of pride and achievement that I have managed to secure tickets to see the match. Fair enough they were acquired through deceit, but all for a good cause I say. I feel even more proud to have given other people the chance to go and hopefully savour the lads winning a crucial promotion in our history.

There is my brother-in-law Al, who at this stage doesn't know if he has enough games under his belt, even though he has been to most away games, as it is very tight with loyalty points. He is safe in the knowledge that he can enjoy his day out, no matter what. Then me dad, who wasn't keen at first, but after sorting the situation, he wants one now. And why not, I owe him a lifetime of favours (and me Mam) so why not get the chance to do something for them for a change.

The final two tickets (Al I'm pretty sure is a prime contender to be invited any-way) will go to my good mates, Ged and Nick. Ged is probably the most ardent Sunderland fan out of the two and has sat through countless disappointments next to me, both home and away. The bastard better not be a bad luck charm again. I've travelled all over the world with Nick, so why not take him on the end of Niall Quinn's carpet sojourn.

And that is my first and last lesson in ticket politics. Everyone is happy.

The Luton gamble is on…

…I have just found out also via the website that the penultimate Burnley home game has been changed. It's now moved from the Saturday (3pm kick off) to the Friday (7.45pm kick off). And the problem? Well seeing as the parents-in-law are visiting us in Cyprus, I've agreed to take them to the Northern side (occupied by Turkey since 1974) of the island for the weekend as part of their holiday.

This means that Friday night sees Dave (my father-in-law) and I finding the near-est local boozer to watch this vital home banker. I could have watched it in the comfort of my own home, had I known well in advance. I have been assured that there are British pubs catering for my requirements. The situation is crazy though, as I can't even phone our hotel to confirm the facility of live football, with any call from the Southern Greek Cypriot side to the Turkish Cypriot side barred, due to the political stance by both nations.

Northern Cyprus is a pretty confusing affair. Turkey claimed it during a civil war, but the Cypriots want it back, plus throw in a United Nations no go buffer zone in between and a border crossing to boot and there are all sorts of madness going on. We will require our passports, so I guess it must be classed as Turkey. That will mean I have watched Sunderland in four countries this season.

August – October – Cyprus
October – February – Afghanistan
27th April (Burnley) – Turkish Republic of Northern Cyprus (Turkey)
6th May (Luton) – United Kingdom
Play-Offs – n/a – hopefully!

Eat your heart out Michael Palin.

Wednesday 28th March 2007

After visiting work to collect any random mail, I notice an internal envelope addressed to my good self. Inside I find my leave pass for the latter part of May (namely the play-off final). A post-it note is crudely stuck on from my boss, offering his sympathies for not authorising my proposed time off, due to lack of manpower. Bollocks. This could border on a major catastrophe. Sure enough I was returning home to see the Luton game, but I still had one worrying eye on the play-off lottery. And knowing Sunderland, they do things the hard way. Combine this fact with the best part of sod's law and I could be grafting, whilst the whole of Wearside and beyond enjoy a taste of Wembley.

Can you imagine how it would feel having to work during Sunderland's most important game in recent history, all unfolding at the extravagant, elegant, breathtaking new London arena. I'd be suicidal; I'd at least be in tears. Now the pressure is really on for the lads to go up automatically. What could I do? Go AWOL? Well I have considered the notion. If I were single, then I'd have no qualms in pursuing my Wembley dream in illegal terms under military law. Now I am married and the prospect of facing military prison in Colchester (at least I'd get to Essex this season) being not good to say the least. It's not the punishment, it would be the drop in wages you face and the possibility of a hefty fine.

Perhaps I could pay for another member of another shift to cover me for the time period required. I'd pay good money, Jon Stead money – over the top wages, possibly for a complete waste of time. The last resort would be to beg and plead with my boss, mind you; AWOL looks favourable compared to that.

Why are things so complicated? Why always to me? And why all through this season?

As I proved with Luton though, I will not give up without a fight. I just pray Keano and the lads won't either. I need a 100% return in form from now, cheers boys.

As for England tonight at Andorra… well I couldn't care less, really.

Thursday 29th March 2007

I have just finished watching that shite – the apparently mighty England against no hopers Andorra. I have witnessed better football down Marley Pots on a Saturday afternoon, or in Thompson Park on a Sunday morning and that is the truth. Only Gerrard had any balls. The rest were awful. In the end I found myself cheering on the underdogs, just in a last ditch attempt to oust the smarmy McClaren. I would have sooner watched Northern Ireland and our own Jonny Evans beat Sweden, it surely would have been more entertaining.

The issue is that I really do not respect half of the England team as human beings. I think in order to represent one's country at any level, at any sport, the individual lucky enough to earn their call up should be of outstanding integrity, demanding respect from all quarters of life. Take for example the Ashley Coles, the Rio Ferdinands and the Frank Lampards. All in my eyes prima donnas, all pampered, all out of touch with reality. And all lacking in effort.

The modern game at this supposed top level is drab. I would rather encounter a slice of guts and determination in the lower leagues. Playing for pride in non-league. Proper football. Perhaps Keano could do the England role in partnership with his Sunderland gaffer's position. To hell with that, we'll keep him to ourselves, thank you very much.

Saturday 31st March 2007 am

I'm not afraid to say that I've never liked Cardiff, be it as a city, the people or the football team and so I don't envy the convoy of Sunderland supporters travelling down to the Welsh capital today. It all stems from one negative experience, revolving around a whole host of individual nightmares.

It was back in February 2004 and in retrospect it would appear as though I were on a suicide mission. Not content with embarking on a sports parachute course, in a bid for two weeks off work, I asked my mate Leigh if he fancied a midweek replay fixture at Birmingham, followed by a weekend in Cardiff. I'm not sure what was the most dangerous, jumping out a dilapidated light aircraft at 3,000 feet, facing the wrath of the Brummie Zulus or daring to speak with an English accent in the heart of Wales?

It proved to be the latter, as from our initial arrival, we were given a lukewarm reception from none other than the B & B landlady, whose property we were acquainting.

"What you here in Cardiff for boys?" cheerily asked our weekend proprietor.

"The football, Cardiff and Sunderland," we answered with confidence.

Well, we might as well have said we were in town to rape and pillage all the local girls whilst looting the vicinity on our way out, judging by the dorsal look on her face and the drop in temperature in the atmosphere. The theme continued as we drank in local bars and clubs minding our own business, with questions of "Are you English?" and frowned looks in our direction. I couldn't believe the sense of anger towards England and the archaic chip on the shoulder small country syndrome, it's something I have come to expect ever since when I've had to visit the place.

The tense situation all came to a head on the match day itself, however if I'm being honest, the travelling contingent did not make matters any better. It just so happened to be the marking of respect of the passing away of a true legend in these parts, John Charles, thus requiring a minute's silence from all areas of the ground. When the tannoy announced this, my heart sank, knowing full well that unfortunately some of our hooligan ranks would deem this as the appropriate opportunity to stoke the Cardiff fires. My suspicions came true.

As the referee's whistle blew to begin the sixty second tribute, the place fell quiet, until ten seconds in the cry of "Sheep shaggers" from one of our lot nearly sparked scenes of riotous proportions from the adjacent shackled home section. Thankfully the safety net took the brunt of the coins and bottles, whilst the barbaric fencing warned off any attack. It was the threats though that broke through, bouncing off most Sunderland fans, giving as good as they got. They though were not here for the weekend. They would soon be on their busses back to more welcoming Northern climes. As for us, we were still rooted in this hostile territory, still having to face the locals.

The football match itself made the weekend more miserable, as Cardiff thumped us 4-0. The home crowd were now pumped up and baying for blood, the Mackems were held back afterwards in an attempt to disperse the waiting mob of Soul Crew and associates. Leigh and I hobbled quietly out the exits, deciding on a quick pint to say our goodbyes, from where he would drive home to Exeter and I would return via train, to my then RAF base at Lyneham, Wiltshire.

The Prince of Wales public house was our choice of alcoholic disembarkation, having being chosen for its modern family appeal. At first glimpse we were correct in our chosen ideologies. Merrily supping away, we were involuntary joined by another Wearside exile, though he turned out to be a loud mouthed obnoxious individual, attracting an ever-growing array of attention from the natives nearby. We knew we had to leave before bother came knocking at our door, but with over three quarters of a pint left, we would finish our lager first.

A moment of grace had come as our new unwanted red and white colleague departed for the toilets. Unfortunately he swiftly reappeared, along with two locals, one an oversized Pancho-looking midget, the other a near on 7ft monster, who would surely tower over the Empire State Building if he gave it as much of a flick.

The midget spoke. "Which one of you is the Sunderland fan with the big mouth?"

Yet again my heart sank. Before I could answer, the monster intervened and arched over me. He bellowed: "We've got forty lads waiting upstairs for you lot if you fancy any trouble, so I suggest you leave if you don't."

For the first time today, the natives and I were in agreement, although I was inclined to inform him how hard they were to congregate a unbalanced ratio of forty to three for a round of fisticuffs, although I thought better of it and ditched my pint, heading straight for the exit instead. Leigh promptly followed, both of us showing a plain disregard for the tosser who put us in this predicament.

And so onto news that my brother-in-law was on his way down to South Wales to cheer on the Lads, I did wonder if I should run a sweepstake on him either being arrested by the local police (who are just as pleasant as their constituency) or receiving a forearm smash from a Bluebird Neanderthal. It was nailed on for City to beat us, so betting on AI getting into trouble seemed a better and more interesting gamble. They were becoming a bogey side, a la Crystal Palace, although we did beat them twice our previous encounters last time out in the Championship.

Jeff Stelling did his best to entertain, keeping spirits up one minute with cries of "constant Sunderland pressure," then doing his utmost to dishearten me to the bowels of my vodka bottle, as "the away side were coming under sustained mounting pressure." One goal would suffice for either team. Thankfully, Ross Wallace obliged with a tame free kick spawning deserved luck, as the keeper scrambled the ball into his own net.

Get in there, class, that'll do for me. I don't care if the ball bounces off the referee's arse, as long as it's a goal, as long as it counts and as long as it's for Sunderland meaning a vital three points, then it's all well and good.

Saturday 31st March 2007 pm

Our lass has received a startling text message from one of her mates from Newcastle. It reads…

"Ow mate niall quinn kicked off easyJet flt 4 bein pissd.flt full of mackems now binnd.ha ha ha."

What the hell was going on here? After further examination, initial reports dictate that an easyJet flight out of Bristol carrying mainly Sunderland fans, fresh from their victory at Cardiff, has been cancelled, due to drunken exploits of the would be passengers. Fuck me, it'll be all over the papers tomorrow, not that I'll have the chance to read them, being a day behind in Cyprus. It can't be true. At least it's not the players then. I suppose Niall can do whatever he likes; after all he is the bloody chairman. It'll all become clear in the morning.

APRIL

Sunday 1st April 2007

Can Niall Quinn become any more of a legend, messiah, god, call it whatever you like? As the truth emerges from various supporters who were on the flight, it transpires that some heavy handed aircraft dispatchers decided to spoil the merriment of the jubilant but law abiding Sunderland supporters. With Quinny sat at one end of the airport bar along with other Sunderland fans (you wouldn't see that at any other club) chants of Niall Quinn's Disco Pants break out on the way to boarding the flight. In this military state of no fun and political correctness, this was deemed the most radical hooligan behaviour by some blinkered trolley dolly, happy to call the local constabulary in an attempt to turf everyone off her aircraft.

Cometh to the rescue Mr Quinn, who intervened with the coppers, smoothed things over with the remaining passengers and promptly organised shed loads of taxis to escort the unwitting victims of injustice back up to the North East homelands. Even those flying without red and white colours were offered the kind gesture, thus costing the club a reported £8,000 bill and easyJet priceless bad publicity and a lesson not to mess with Mackems.

Amidst varied rumours of the circumstances surrounding the whole affair, it appears that Sunderland AFC and Quinny in particular have come up trumps once again. Whoever was to blame for this ramshackle disaster, which involved disabled fans being ejected from their seats, Sir Niall saves the day once more. Maybe one day Sunderland City Council may even have the decency to honour the great man with the freedom of the City of Sunderland.

Friday 7th April 2007

I've been too depressed to write all week. Don't quite know what the matter is. I'm back at work, still thinking of Afghanistan, the stress of following Sunderland's turbulent promotion run in from afar. It is all boiling under. I even visited the doctor this week. She recalled high blood pressure on one test, but my headaches were put down to stress.

She filled my head of routine scenarios, involving my four-month stint in the Middle East, but I longed to inform her that I supported Sunderland AFC and if there was anything she could do to calm my nerves and aid sleepless nights. True, my time away was chaotic and mentally challenging. Though watching from afar with heightened anticipation over our final few games of the season was now pushing me over the edge.

Enter the prescription phase of the conversation and the salvation of sleeping pills.

"Just enough to ease you back into sleep," she softly spoke and so I was slightly concerned to read that I'd been prescribed Temazepam. Wasn't this stuff for heroin addicts, or some homeless junkie, escaping the pain of reality? Then it hit me. I am in some sense a junkie myself. An addict of the beautiful game, desperate to catch glimpses of analysis, league tables, news roundups, Ceefax headlines, football gossip, Halifax versus Oxford live on Sky on a Monday evening. The week old Football Echoes, fantasy leagues, Soccer Saturday, internet spiel, fans' opinions, match day programmes, fixture run ins, opposition web sites, Soccer AM, ticket details (whether I'm attending or not), travel itineraries, match statistics, You're On Sky Sports, fanzines – national and club level, official merchandise, terrace chants rattling around my brain, banter with the lads, the red and white cloth, the weekend football accumulator, even practising pre-match drinking habits and ordering obscure memorabilia over the net (one Forres Mechanics Highland League scarf and one Gretna v. Derry City UEFA Cup scarf) for the Red and White Tractor bar. It all comes to a head... pass me the pills.

I've only been handed a week's worth to quell my sorrows, but I won't have one tonight, as I'm at work in the morning and will probably drive into a plane knowing my luck, making Operation Cuckoo a wasted effort.

I decide to celebrate my acquisition of sleeping tablets by having a classic Roy Keane haircut, with a number four all over the order of the day. Choices for barbers are limited in Cyprus. There is no Fellaz as per Sea Road, Fulwell, notorious for the football craic and no John's à la Sunderland City centre, steeped in quality banter. There is a Toni and Guy in Limmasol centre for the wannabe third division footballers in the area. The top one for sheer ease and located two minutes away, belongs to a local called Nick. He is an aging Cypriot trying to relieve the retro years, sporting a Bjorn Bjorg image, complete with minimalist white leather jacket, plain grey shirt and dress trousers.

In the background the wireless receiver spits out some kind of religious prayers in tinny mono effect, which endure hypnotising side effects, gently easing me into a trance, reminiscent of a hill top somewhere in Arabia. Who needs drugs now? I'm soon brought back to life by the sight of his cutthroat razor hovering towards my ears, whilst I gently remind him that I've seen Reservoir Dogs, so don't be pulling any stunts. His nails are vampire like, starting to curl at the ends, most akin to pig trotters cum eagle claws. Am I going round the twist? My orders of a Keano number are obviously ignored as Nick shaves my whole head, bar a tuft at the front, which he assures me "looks good blended in."

I'm too weary of his deathly prowl and walk out of his shop bearing the image of a Zinedine Zidane/Bob Murray devil spawn on my head. I have stuck with it for now, until someone notices.

Anyway, I digress. My Dad informs me of his two-hour torment, waiting in the ticket office queue, trying to obtain tickets for the forthcoming Southampton game at St Mary's on Monday. These are for my cousin and her two boys who live in Bournemouth. It's the bairns' first ever game, so I'm pleased two more of my exiled family pledge their allegiance to the red and white cause and football in general. He was only waiting for this game, but the old man tells me tales of long lines of people wanting both new season tickets for next year and for today's Easter Friday game against Wolves. It seems as though happy days are here again and finally fans are starting to dare to believe again. And I'm happy… most of all for Niall Quinn. His spirit, generosity and genius has been rewarded, by those who love him the most.

My old man attended today's game, Mick McCarthy's first visit back to the SOL since his sacking from the club, last season. Dad nabbed one of our neighbours' spare season tickets. The wise old football connoisseur told of his enjoyment, while I grafted away in the Cyprus heat, eager to hear of any news filtering through. One of the other lads is a Wolves fan, so the stakes were high to ascertain who had the bragging rights on the shift. I needn't have worried as Daryl Murphy and Ross Wallace produced the goals as we ran out 2-1 victors. Absolutely chuffed to bits and doubly so as rivals Brum were upstaged at home to Burnley, 0-1. Brucey will be doing his nut. Derby drew yesterday to leave us in the automatic places, this time hopefully to stay.

I spend the remainder of my Saturday night locked on the internet, analysing all reports and match quotes. Needless to say, I won't require my Temazepams tonight. Keano and the lads have eased my nightmares.

Monday 9th April 2007

I can't stop looking at the Championship league table. It's quality, sublime, class, mint, joyful and the rest. Absolutely incredible, Sunderland are top of the league. The Easter weekend could not have been kinder. All the big boys dropped points, apart from ourselves. I still can't fathom out, never mind accept the events which have unfolded this holiday break.

It all could have been so different. My freeview box card keeps reminding me that my subscription to the service is coming to an end, even though it is paid for by the Armed Forces. I suspected it to be a card error and chose to ignore the imperative demands of renewal. It wasn't until the missus stated that even though there was no cost, the card itself still needed renewing. As it was the Easter holidays, the TV place was closed, leading me to paranoid fears that the thing would decide to expire at a crucial stage in today's game with Southampton. You can imagine the frustration. Anyhow, it worked, and to great effect.

Suffering from a poignant hangover, I resorted to good old English tea for kick off as I watched, perched on my sofa for the late evening kick off at St Mary's. This choice of fluid soon developed into a bout of Californian Cabernet Sauvignon, my grape of choice to muster the required energy in confronting a match of this order and importance. The first half saw both teams and me on knife-edge, with neither side settling on the ball. Sunderland though did have the better of the play, hitting the post through David Connolly, whilst Stephen Elliott was a constant pain in the arse for the home defence.

The second half saw Sunderland pissing about with the ball, as Southampton took advantage of our sloppy play. This somewhat infuriated one watching Mackem, as the paint began to fester away from the walls of my living room, with my expletive language changing from adolescent purple to deep graphic blue.

As I rushed into the kitchen to dip into the wine reinforcements, a gasp is heard from the wife and Southampton have scored – bollocks. Needless to say, I hit the roof and, shortly after, the bottle.

Sunderland never looked like scoring in a month of Sundays, never keeping possession long enough to pose a threat. I really did think that was it, our long unbeaten run over and we'd fluffed the chance to go top. Yet one half of me felt the Keane Empire Effect, the never say die spirit, which would be a benefactor of Wearside.

It is a strange sensation to have on your side. And so when Carlos Edwards cut inside and unleashed a rocket shot into the top corner of the net, I was ecstatic, my voice reverberating around the walls of my house. A goal like that, out of nothing, in my opinion is the greatest. True, last minute winners are awe inspiring, but to score a goal out of nothing is greater still, it's unexpected. To have a second then was beyond belief. Connolly runs rings around the home defence, lays a pass off to Grant Leadbitter, who takes a touch and wallop – a curling shot into the other side of the net. Fuck me I'm on the ceiling now, pride bursting out of my body, the summit of the league awaits.

Out came my camera, which I have incorporated into my match day practice, hoping to capture the decisive moments of Sunderland's march to glory, even if it is via TV. This comes with much annoyance from the wife, indicating my ridiculous sadness once more. For now I can't sit still waiting for the referee's final jolt of his whistle. I'm akin to a speed addict, who has recently indulged in their latest dab of the narcotic white powder.

Finally the whistle is blown to signal the rise and rise of Sir Roy Keane. From second bottom to top of the league in 37 league games, in what some describe as the hardest league in the world to escape from.

Stunning, bloody stunning. My gamble of Luton away looks inspired at the moment. Long may it continue.

Tuesday 10th April 2007

Reading A Love Supreme's website this morning, it is revealed that once again the club has come to the rescue of their travelling fans. Apparently stone age Saints fans stung by the 2-1 defeat in the final quarter of the match, decided to hurl bricks and the like at the Sunderland coaches en route for home as they left the stadium.

One coach was deemed as being no longer roadworthy, as local police allowed the other its long arduous journey to continue. The victimised bus was taken away, thus leaving more stranded followers.

As the players and coaching staff were flying back up to the North East, the team bus was driving back empty and so it made sense for the nomadic hordes in red and white to rest their hardy souls, celebrating the summit of the Championship in style. Another classic example of bonding between supporter and club. Another example of what the new Quinn-inspired regime brings to our aspirations. This would not have happened under Fickling and Murray.

After the taxi parade last week and now this act of salvation in our midst, rumours were rife that Niall was trying in vain to find a buyer for the ailing flagship city centre store, Joplings, which is facing closure. My Mam would be grateful, although I don't want to get her hopes up.

Tuesday 17th April 2007

It is Birmingham's game in hand tonight, away to Leicester. All the media talk is centred around all the permutations and events that can unfold, should they lose. I fully expect the fuckers to win, to keep the pressure on, but I suppose Keane would have it no other way. A Leicester win would be fantastic though…

…after a lucky pint of Guinness, Birmingham are 2-0 up after twenty minutes – shit. I turn off the ceefax vidiprinter in frustration, choosing instead the works of Stanley Kubrick and his horror flick The Shining. The one where Jack Nicholson, the would be writer, goes insane through the stress of being alone, finally going mad, producing pages of lunacy. It's a cruel brain cluster fuck to play, in a bid to counteract the temazzies, but it's gone seriously wrong…

All work and no football makes me a sad man. All work and no football makes me a sad man. All work and no football makes me a sad man. All work and no football makes me a sad man. All work and no football makes me a sad man. All work and no football makes me a sad man. All work and no football makes me a sad man. All work and no football makes me a sad man. All work and no football makes me a sad man. All work and no football makes me a sad man. All work and no play makes me a sad boy. All work and no football makes me a sad man. All work and no football makes me a sad lad. All work and no play makes me a sad man. All work and no football makes me a sad man. All work and no football makes me a sad man. All work and no promotion makes me mad. All work and no play makes me a sad man. All work and no football makes me a sad man. All work and no football makes me a sad man. All work and no football makes me a sad man. All work and no football makes me a sad man. All work and football makes me a sad man. All work and no football makes me a sad man. All work, all work, all work, all work, all work, all work, all work, all work, work ,work, work, work, work, work…aaaaaaarrrrrrrrrrgggggghhhhhhhh!

Now I know how he felt. Poor bastard. At least I've forgotten about Birmingham for now.

Saturday 14th April 2007

I decide to engage in a new line of approach for the home game against Queens Park Rangers today. After increasing levels of stress, resulting from various sources, I take advantage of my mate Spit's free stay in one of the five star hotels in Limassol Bay. He is there for the weekend and invited us down on the sly, to share the wealth with the luxury of the complex facilities.

I agreed to join him on the principle that if Roy Keane were a professional football supporter, rather than player or manager then this methodical, professional warm up would be right up his street.

As fans trudge into their local boozer, high on nerves, fingernails bitten to the core, I'm sat soaking in the early summer sun, casually dipping in the ice cube pool, before taking in a three course buffet option (courtesy of Spit's hangover meaning no food for him today) and relaxing in the jacuzzi. There I am living the life of a professional footballer, all I require are the surroundings of the SOL dressing room, the banter of the players (I imagine Anthony Stokes and Dwight Yorke to be the leaders of the pack here) and the coolness of the gaffer, Royston Keane.

It's then that the daydream falters, but I'm not complaining as the endless jacuzzi bubbles wear away the aches, stresses and pains (both mental and physical) of the season so far. Now I'm ready. Now I'm on top form, ready to cheer the lads on to glory. My newfound energy is somewhat quashed at the sight of the time and the signal to return home to get ready for night shift. Bugger…

…a quiet night means that my day at the hotel isn't wasted. I still miss the final scores, but I am consoled with a narrow 2-1 home victory. Skipper Dean White-head and Grant Leadbitter steal the glory with the two Sunderland goals.

There was some slight concern, after one of the lads passed a false scoreline of an away lead and in truth I should know better, but this bastard could keep a straight face even if Ken Dodd was tickling his bollocks with a feather duster. My anxiety was eased only after ceefax had sorted itself out. I felt rather perturbed at the screen's incarnation of S%$derla*nd 2 Shrews&ury Ha"rie+s 4. The devil's transcript gently unravelled to reveal the truth of a hearty three points for the lads.

Perhaps the delights of the high life should be enjoyed every Saturday. I doubt if our lass would agree, considering our current financial shortcomings. Luton draws nearer, though.

On return home later that evening, the news of Sunderland's latest victory was heralded further, as Derby conspire to lose 2-1 at Ipswich, with the gap between automatic and the play-off spaghetti junction increasing. Fair enough, Birming-ham have a game in hand, but we are now four points clear of the Rams. I keep hearing of the commentators and pundits exasperating about our incredible unbeaten run this year, however I feel none of us will appreciate just what an effort it was, maybe until the end of the season, successful or not.

Sunday 15th April 2007

Still revelling in our top of the table status, I find myself staring at the league table in disbelief, or is it sheer amazement? Here we are with three games left and we're sitting pretty. Yet in the true style of a pro, I'll have to comment that nothing's won yet.

I keep harbouring thoughts that Sunderland will blow it all away, as only we can. This time though my doubts are aggravated by Keano's chilling winning mental-ity, ruthless, calm and relaxed persona.

On top of the playing side, all the quotes and murmurs coming from inside the club are as positive as Mark Fowler's HIV diagnosis. Quinny announcing that over

20,000 season tickets have now been sold for next season, regardless of what division we find ourselves in. Then Sir Niall adds talk of Keane's current contract and the possibility of a lengthy extension. Then Roy responds stating he would be happy to stay for the long haul, his family are settled in the area, despite the strong North East gusts. News of a considerable transfer war chest for next year and everything is rosy in the garden of Sunderland.

To have a board and manager in unison, sharing the same vision, is quite surreal. You see, something this simple just hasn't happened to us in recent history. It is absurd really, we've waited this long, but now the moment has finally arrived, I will bathe in its glory and bask in its brilliance.

The new Sunderland AFC – ambition in motion, so it seems.

Saturday 21st April 2007

Don't really feel like writing. We've just been beaten for the first time in 2007 to bloody Colchester – the little upstarts. And I've just run out of cold beer.

I'm still only mildly irritated though, not totally despondent. As Keano says you can't win every match, but this is still a kick in the bollocks, when it happens. And to Colchester (this may sound arrogant, petty and childish), why don't they ball off back to the lower leagues? Trying to nitpick their way through this division, with the ground the size of a gnat's cock. It's a joke really. Health and safety, anyone?

I don't mean it really, just getting the defeat out of my system – you bastards.

Still if Wolves beat Birmingham tomorrow, everything will remain the same, everything sorted and on course for the Championship trophy, although second place will suffice at this nervy moment in time.

I've been at work all day, only finishing halfway through the first half, in which I would have settled for the draw. But on seeing that our lass had placed a bet on Sunderland to win (meaning instant bad luck) and the fact that Tony Cottee was reporting (the West Ham old boys network lover, with never a good word to say about us, never mind see us win) meant that we never stood a chance from kick off. The cockney pundit was even there when Birmingham equalized in the last minute at St Andrews in March and he was present at Roots Hall, Southend, when the Shrimpers beat us 3-1 in August. Not a good omen then, it would be safe to say.

I have decided that watching Soccer Saturday is similar to flying in a passenger airliner. For one you have no control (a big contributor to fear of flying) and secondly, you can't see where you're heading, or for that matter, what's coming. Added to these combined factors is the illusion of Jeff Stelling, playing on both positive and negative emotions, connecting the two like an alkaline battery, but always resulting in the steady pace of your heart. Take for example today.

"There's been a penalty at Layer Road," with the home side currently 2-1 to the good. The adrenaline kicks in and inadvertently deflates after seconds of apprehension and hope, which give way to depreciation accompanying the news of a confirmed third goal for Colchester.

I'm too disgruntled to write anymore, but I've taken defeat on the chin, like a true football fan – whinging and moaning all through the evening's aftermath.

If we win the final two games – we are up! Keep it simple, stupid.

Sunday 22nd April 2007

I'm sitting in the guardroom on camp, feeling depressed. I'm on a station duty, otherwise known as Duty Runner, which basically entails me manning the office for 24 hours, performing all sorts of weird and wonderful dogs body type of tasks.

As today is Sunday though, things around the place are quiet. This probably makes the chore of this role even worse. I can't leave the room for 24 hours, except to perform my duties. I'm a prisoner in this bland, blank room, with only a small TV, fridge and kettle for company. At least the TV is equipped with the satellite freeview card à la my house.

The Flight Sergeant I'm on with is football mad too, admitting to officiating at local games, the crazy fool. Thank God, I could think of nothing worse than spending 24 hours locked away with a non-footballite. Now that would be plain insane. I am struggling to stay awake and focussed around mid day. I can only imagine what state I'll be in come midnight or shift handover in the morning. There is a feast of football on the box though, with Wolves versus Birmingham being the highlight of the day for me. Here's hoping for a victory for Mick McCarthy and the boys in gold…

…the game has just finished. If I thought I was depressed before, I'm cemented in the doldrums of despair now. The Blue half of this Midlands derby have shaded a narrow victory, 3-2, to knock Sunderland off top spot. Even Wolves conspired to miss a penalty in the last minute. I'm raging, not helped by the fact the Flight Sergeant, a Villa fan, is loving every minute of watching me squirm, as if my own suffering is some kind of twisted personal entertainment for him, relieving his clock watching on shift for a few hours.

I had a few jobs to perform during the match, promptly leaving the office as Birmingham drew first blood. On arrival back, I was overjoyed to see Wolves 2-1 up with quarter of an hour remaining. Get in there; we've been spared, after the damning defeat yesterday. Wrong, Brum scored, apparently as soon as I left the vicinity and then once more, within minutes of my arrival back. I even suggested I go back out the room to turn Wolves' (and our) fortunes around, me being an obvious bad luck charm. I was even offered the chance to venture outside when Wolves were awarded their doomed spot kick, but no, I stayed and watched in horror.

Heaven knows I'm miserable now.

I try to concentrate on the remainder of the Premiership fare on offer on television, but my mind is strangely elsewhere. One minute we were up, the next kicked in the swingers, left hanging by a thread. Promotion though is still in our hands, even if the title may not be. The Blues do have to play in-form Preston in Lancashire if that's any consolation.

I clutch on to the fact that my vision of Carlos Edwards, slotting a crucial winner away in time added on at Kenilworth Road in two weeks, as Birmingham and Derby only draw, to send the away end into delirium and us four pretend Hatters bonkers, still remains true in my focus. The Championship trophy is paraded and although it is only a replica (with the football league presuming that City have the upper hand, thus despatching the original trophy to Deepdale) it was still celebrated with elation mixed with disbelief at a side never knowing when they've been beaten.

Well that is how I would like things to emerge. For now, I'm tired, hacked off and want to bury myself far away from reality for a few hours. End of story.

Monday 23rd April 2007

I'm still awake… just. My eyes are dried out, enraged with the bleach effect of constant burning. My teeth are as furry as a nun's bush, complimenting my stained teacher's breath of copious amounts of coffee and tea. It smells like someone has shat out a bucket load of arsepiss into my gob, all the pleasures of 24 hour duty at work. Not nice, I don't feel good, trying in vain to forget all about this woeful weekend.

I bet all the fucking dickheads working out the promotion premonitions and permutations of the promotion scenario at the weekend are quiet today. People never learn. It is never over with Sunderland until Iain Hesford sings.

I'm off to bed to nurse my sporting comedown.

Wednesday 25th April 2007

I awoke today to hear news that the SOL had been on fire. Our lass's dad informed her at work. It had me frantically phoning home in search of the exact details. Turns out my father knew nothing about it!

After sifting through the internet and Ceefax, I found out it was only restricted to the director's suite and that the all-important Friday night game with Burnley can go ahead.

There's me having visions of a possible postponed game, or incredibly switching venues. Imagine the game that could see Sunderland promoted (depending on other results) being played out at St James or the Riverside Stadium? There would be outrage and the sheer thought of it sends a shiver down my spine.

Niall Quinn probably extinguished the flames alone, seeing as he has done everything else off the pitch for our club this season.

Friday 27th April 2007

My parents-in-law arrived on Wednesday for a week's holiday and as promised a three-day jaunt into the uncharted territory of Turkey's Northern Cyprus, beginning today.

I'm no historical expert on why there are two separate nations on one island, however I believe it had something to do with the Turkish invasion of Cyprus in and around 1974. What I do know is that there is still bad blood between the two countries, so far to the extent that in Cyprus they won't even sell the confectionary Turkish Delight, opting for the more homely Cyprus Delight instead. I am not a politician and so no slants on the miniscule details of the rights and wrongs of the whole affair from me. All I want to do is to explore this peculiarly titled land, a somewhat hidden gem, just to say I've been there, to wear that metaphorical t shirt and drink their beer.

Tonight Sunderland are entertaining Burnley at home live on Sky Sports, in what has to be one of our biggest home games in years. Forget the play off semi-final under McCarthy, in which we were controversially beaten by Palace. Forget games against Sheffield United in the quarter final of the F.A Cup, forget the Mags, Boro, Manchester United et al. Taking in all the previous recent history, including the two mournful seasons in the top flight, in which a tee total could have accumulated more drink driving points than our league accumulation, the chance to bounce straight back into the face of Premiership adversity is phenomenal. The chance to wipe away those embarrassments once and for all under a new dawn is now. Therefore putting this match at the pinnacle of critical significance in our modern times. Hopefully, the lads will grab this opportunity with both feet and have us all dancing in the streets, Wearside, Northern Cyprus, the Bermuda Triangle, it all counts, we're all Mackems worldwide.

And so we set off on our maiden voyage into lands unknown. The journey time is an expected three hour drive, depending on the queue at the border crossing. I put my faith in my decrepit Nissan Pulsar (really an Almera), hopefully drawing from some Wearside maintenance at some stage of its life. In my mind I know it will be touch and go if we arrive over the border, but as far as everyone else is concerned, the navigation will be the main source of irritation on this route. I say irritation, with our lass at the helm of the atlas. Fortunately for us all, her work colleague had journeyed the same trek a week earlier, passing explicit instruction down to the miniscule detail.

The only cause for confusion along the way resulted in our party of four nearly on the receiving end of sporadic gunfire, as we tried to surface through an unregulated checkpoint, with the missus adding "it was a mistake anyone could make." We sought courage from our second coming and proceeded onwards towards the official border control.

This was all new to me. The only time I had previously passed through countries via land was from Holland into Germany and then I was only a wee nipper. To trigger a border crossing in mainland Europe would be akin to driving past a curry house in Bradford. To do so on a remote island perched in the middle of the Mediterranean Sea, well that was different.

I expected armed guards and their ilk. In their place were helpful Cypriots from both sides, one to arrange new car insurance for the duration of our stay in the North, one to fill out a paper issue visa and one to search anything suspicious, although this was reserved mainly for the passage back into Southern Cyprus, thanks to the cheap fags, amongst other tradable items found in the Turkish vicinity.

I admit I was wary and nervous about treading foot over the borderline. For one if the car gave way and conked out, there was no AA to bail us out, with our Greek Cypriot number plates hardly an invitation to Turkish do-gooders driving by ready to tow us all the way to our lodgings. Secondly, the old adage of the fear of the unknown rears its ugly head again. Not content with one outing this season, thanks to the conflicts in Afghanistan, the air of pastures new proved to be a precarious topic, within the realms of the Pulsar.

As we gathered our paperwork for the Turkish Republic of Northern Cyprus, I drove apprehensively past the guards, into the UN no go buffer zone, effectively a no man's land. Green turf coarsen into overgrown weeds, ordinary buildings dwindled into derelict obsolete skeletons. What the fuck has happened and is happening here?

I drive on with caution, unaware that the road signs have disorientated from the bog standard English type, now reading in full Turkish dialect. The traffic lights follow suit, switching to full blown flashing orange bollocks. I drive straight through; these alien signals mean nothing to me. We follow the directions given like a trainee doctor scrutinising the schematics of their first operational procedures. This barren land epitomises my initial appraisals. The place looks outdated, shanty bars lined with over-populated residencies.

The linear road now bends up a mountain. Rock climbers of imperial standards would struggle, never mind the poor crumbling Pulsar, which at this time had decided to perform boy racing screeches every time I applied the brakes, or turned a corner. Come on baby, we're nearly there.

Just when things seem to be going under, the endless gradient of the mountain gives way to a pulsating descent, just as rapid as the climb, to reveal the seaside resort of Kyrenia, enveloped in full scope beneath us. A hidden gem? More like an untouched goldmine of a choice. The excursion hadn't finished though. As we rambled our way through all the niceties of the welcoming coastal bay, I continued to put the Pulsar through unrelenting paces by driving back up mountainous peaks towards the safe haven of our hotel. We'd arrived in the hilly tropics of Northern Cyprus. The views were spectacular, now open the bar and bring on the football…

…to keep everyone happy, we've all arranged to pop out to the local harbour to sample the local cuisine, mindful that the imminent kick off is approaching. On the way past all the typical tourist locations, our party encounter numerous invites to the various eateries on offer. I make a pact.

"If you tell us what bars have got the match on, we'll eat in your restaurant," I bargained.

I was slightly alarmed by the response of "what match?" by not one but several bemused Turks.

"The main match, Sunderland against Burnley, tonight on Sky. Which bars have Sky?" I pleaded.

Eventually, a fisherman came to my aid, pointing out several bars, including upmarket hotels, which would probably show the game. Quality, we'd have some scran, knock it down the hatch with a few beers and shots of local liqueur and off to cheer the lads on.

Everything went to plan, with our hosts even producing the food in quick succession in order for us to be on our way within half an hour. The bill was paid, our gratitude handed out in abundance. It then went more pear shaped and tits up than a bunch of Dolly Parton's hand picked ripened beauties.

On arrival at every bar sworn to be showing the live game between Sunderland and Burnley, we were met with dismissive looks. One after the other we were turned away, until it all rested on one, a sure cert to be showing the football. It was after all an English owned bar, reminiscent of a former Embassy colonial building, perfect for the atmospheric match temper in these circumstances.

"No match on tonight lads," came the response.

"It's Sunderland on tonight marra!" I insisted.

"Yeah we know, but Friday nights are karaoke and they'll go spare if it's not on." The barman acknowledges the punters, wavering his finger towards a crowd of two loyal singers.

It is now two minutes until kick off and I'm beyond fuming.

"Right, everyone back to the hotel, they've got Sky in the bar," I instruct the others, the father-in-law in full recognition of my orders.

We hail a taxi, but the hotel is another fifteen minutes away, resulting in me mumbling to myself all the way, shaking my head in disbelief.

"Of all the matches, of all the fucking places," I rage in the back of the cab.

The others are silent apart from Davey, trying in earnest to calm my fits of anger. After a torturous return journey back to our digs, we dash to the bar, to witness the final nail in the fucking coffin. The TVs are all switched off, but the residents are not, now in full party mode, as George Michael belts out his greatest hits through the bar stereo.

"Have you not got the match on?" I now shout over choruses of Careless Whisper.

It turns out it is disco night at the bar and so the match can only be shown without sound. Bollocks, but that'll do for now, until I barter some more, at a later stage. Well, in about ten minutes sharp to be precise.

On goes the small portable TV, to reveal the score of 1-0 to Sunderland.

Get in there me bonny lads. However no sooner as I had finished the final syllable of lads had Darren Ward raced off his line and brought down the Burnley forward for an immediate spot kick decision from the referee. I don't believe it, even more gutting is that Andy Gray, the ex-Sunderland striker who couldn't score in the Blue Monkey, or the Premiership, stepped up to slot home the equaliser, giving the old wind up celebration to the North Stand. It brought a reaction from those present, as well as those in this Northern Cyprus hotel bar. I was soon told to climb down off my bar stool by the manager, who then offered free shots by way of kind gesture for me toeing the line. This was necked on the news that David Connolly had already missed one penalty earlier in the half, only showed to us just before half time, obviously on mute. I don't believe this.

As the half time whistle blew, so too did I under the constant pressure of a mounting crescendo of more George Michael. I flipped my lid, insisting that I was off to bed, as there was no point in trying to watch Sunderland's biggest game in years without sound. It wasn't about enjoying the match, as I don't think I would be able to do so with or without surround sound commentary. I solely required sound to aid my concentration, in my singular lonesome attempt to urge the lads onto victory, so engrossed I was, at this stage of the season. As I gazed around the bar once more to survey the melee of the remnants from the jovial sing song, I noticed only two couples remained, themselves on the last dregs of their final drink. I gave the bar tender another "Ha'way marra, play the game" plea, to see if the hotel policy on anti-football had changed.

To my surprise, the local staff agreed that everyone had heard enough Wham! for the night and both TVs came alive to the second half roar, fresh from the bowels of the SOL. I would recognise that almighty call anywhere. The amalgamation of incessant noise, chants of "Red and White army," overlapped by renditions of The Beatles' Hey Jude, now concocted to hear the lyrics of "Na na na na, Keano." I was somewhere new, somewhere completely obscure, yet the familiarisation of the match day choir, from the shores of home, instantly melted my temper, and I was back in the heart of my native land.

I was now back in full football mode, watching my team, beer in hand, heart in mouth. It was soon to shoot through the roof of my skull, as an onrushing Burnley midfielder tried a speculative shot, which in mid air changed into wonder strike, to nestle in the top corner of the home goal. Bastards.

My annoyance and anxiety returned in droves, with orders now placed at top shelf status behind the bar. Would this be one hurdle too far for Sunderland? I had new belief since the arrival of Roy Keane, but maybe luck was not on our side. Nah, sod that, winners make their own luck and that's what we'll do. Come on me bonny lads.

Within minutes of my inner resolve shining through, so too did the team, making their own luck, as Sunderland were awarded their second penalty of the night. On this occasion it was a definite foul, unlike the previous two for both sides. Whilst delighted with the decision, fear took hold of my body, immediately from the first blowing of the referee's whistle. Fair play, David Connolly had some balls to step up to take another penalty. Was it to be sheer bravery or sheer lunacy?

The ball hit the back of the net in slow motion, with the bar staff joining in with our own celebrations, serving up more alcohol to flood the mind and quell the nerves. This is it, now we motor on.

Every tackle, every pass is re-enacted out in the bar, as both the father-in-law and I kick every ball up for grabs. The game is virtually end-to-end and by far the most entertaining I've seen all season. The crowd are in the mood too, belting out choruses of approval, battling for every ball themselves.

Then the moment arrives. In a slick counter attack, the ball is played out of the defence to Hysen, then Daryl Murphy, cut inside to Edwards, who is allowed a run at goal, eventually unleashing a belter of a shot, arrowed into the top corner of the Burnley goal. In tandem, Davey and I reach for the sky arms aloft, no doubt awaking the early sleepers in the rest of the establishment. Once more the bar staff cheer along, now all fully in tune to the dramas of this epic battle. What a beauty, I console myself as images of Keano's clenched fists on the touchline are matched by Quinny's rage of joy in the stands, relayed in time with replays of Edwards' scorching strike. Unbelievable, almost unreal.

The ten minutes eat away at my internal nervous system like a fly spray, inflicting serious corrosive damage to its victim. Fingernails are non-existent, they disappeared in March sometime. I'm now down to the fifth layer of skin, as I gnaw away, frantically screaming for the final chapter to conclude on this turbulent match.

Ultimately the referee's whistle is heard through the crowd's high-pitched imitations, to signal an overwhelming sense of pride and elation. Davey and I swerve towards our pints, finding salvation in the nourishment of beer, thus steadying the shattered stress levels and cooling the tortured minds. We rest on the bar, as if we'd played the ninety minutes ourselves. Every emotion was encountered, leaving two drained men, limping away into the night, savouring the sweetest of victories to be talked about the following morning.

I was drunk on sensation, intoxicated with passion, fuelled by pride and a gigantic three points towards the promised land of the Premiership.

Later that night, I once again took a TV photo for me to look back on and recall this momentous victory. It was an interview of our saviour Roy Keane, in a pre-recorded after match analysis. It was through Sky News; I captured the great man's face, also recording whatever the headlines of the day were underneath. Just by chance the caption read "Al Qaeda operative detained by US."

This made me chuckle, whilst somehow displaying a sense of irony, perhaps fate conjured up. In a season in which I travelled to the deserts of the Middle East, I return to see my beloved football team on the march to glory, maybe as a reward for my sacrifices. Now plain to see in all its glory. Even Keano wouldn't allow these extremists in his way, as his Empire Effect envelopes everyone connected with our club, re-issuing life through the veins of our support.

God save the Keane.

Saturday 28th April 2007

Holiday mood was well and truly entered the following day. Flashbacks from the previous night's drama only reinforced the positive feeling, dining on fine food at the breakfast table, overlooking the juggernaut iconic mountains in one sector, the inviting turquoise waters spread out down below. Life is good today. A swim in the Arctic-like pool, followed by a jaunt up the mountain to observe hilltop Turkish villages, whilst reminiscing on Carlos Edwards' pearler, Sunderland's season so far and what of the forthcoming fixtures later on in the day.

It was like an insight into World Cup tournament schedules, in which the players resting from the night before stroll around chatting tactics and formulas. We could have been former players (Davey and I) or coaches, surveying the campaign to date, taking in the cultural delights of unspoilt land.

Anyway, I digress. We return from the splendours of our walk, ready to settle straight into the realms of a pint, watching from afar, today's edition of Soccer Saturday. For once, the pressure is absent, Jeff Stelling's wind-ups are amusing and Chris Kamara is entertaining as ever.

It would be nice if Birmingham were beaten today, although not disastrous if they won, after all I am now convinced Sunderland have done enough to earn promotion. Last night was a pivotal moment, one of the greatest to be played out at the SOL, and football is the greatest game in the world.

This statement was only compounded further watching the fall from grace of Leeds United. Today was the day, after a pitch invasion, they were finally relegated to the third tier of English football. Hard to imagine for their fans is that times like these are to be taken on the chin, not doubting the fact that their fall will be followed by a rise, à la Sunderland and the era of Denis Smith in 1987/88. Football has no regard for reputations, however a club's fortunes can change in an instant, again ironic in the fact that it could well have been us invading the pitch and not the regulars at Elland Road, if not for the intervention of Quinn and Keane.

Birmingham win against Sheffield Wednesday, meaning only a Derby slip up at Crystal Palace tomorrow will elevate both Sunderland and Birmingham, without kicking a ball. Palace do us a favour, I don't think so. My Luton gamble looks inspired. Only a week now until the smell of the lush green of the pitch, the tingle of the match atmosphere and anticipation of promotion. Bring it on.

Sunday 29th April 2007

Our final day in the Turkish Republic of Northern Cyprus sees more sun worshipping by our party, submitting to the rays from above in an effort to turn brown, only for it to wash off on setting foot on English soil. I face the drawn out drive back, praying for good luck on my return in the Pulsar.

On the descent back towards the Western linked Southern side, I noticed a small-scale football ground. I know Cyprus itself is backward when it comes to talent and facilities on display on a football pitch, but what about the residing Turks in this province? I remember reading an article based on the Alternative World Cup in which all the states, countries and subsidiaries in various continents do battle against each other, as they are not recognised by FIFA – the world's governing body. Teams such as Greenland, Tibet and even Afghanistan are reported to have graced this area, with Northern Cyprus the host country. Now that would have been some football story to tell the grandchildren. Tibet versus Greenland, akin to watching The Grindon Mill against The Millers Inn.

As I daydream away the journey home, I notice the impending UN buffer zone, signalling the approach to the border crossing. No parking or photography here, the road signs clearly state. You'd be knackered if you were a member of the paparazzi in a broken down vehicle. Both sides of the border would have your balls on a string in such unfortunate circumstances. I'm dribbling on, but I don't care. This has been the first taste of freedom, away from the shackles of the every day promotional run in. Today feels different, like a weight off my shoulders, a foot taken off my head, drowning underwater. I'll be watching Derby later on, sipping on the cold comforts of Warsteiner, but I won't become aggravated or maligned. I shall sit back and enjoy the comfort zone of being in control of our own destiny, regardless of the final score. Meanwhile, I'm disturbed from my inner soul-searching by the customs man, wanting to search my vehicle and bags on arrival back into Cyprus. I assure him I have no fags and we're on our way…

…my promises of no aggravagation or bad temperedness go haywire, with minutes remaining of the match between Palace and Derby. Astonishingly, the Eagles have just bagged a second goal, thanks to none other than Republic of Ireland international Clinton Morrison, and I'm jumping all over Davey, messing his hair, depicting his bald spot. Still my anguish ignites, expletives dotted around in conversation, ordering Palace to keep possession, even at this late stage.

The County fans are quiet, distraught with the loneliness of the one team to narrowly miss out on automatic promotion. I on the other hand am ecstatic, bouncing up and down, like a big daft kid who has just won the year off school. As the clock ticks down, attentions of the Sky cameras turn to the crowd and in particular, one happy Sunderland fan, perched on his seat, deep in the home end mixing with the Palace contingent, slaps on the back all around. Fair play son, I'd have done the same given the opportunity, although there was potential room at the start to look like a tit if Derby had won. His gamble had worked.

The final whistle displayed abject Rams followers. In the confines of this daft lad's living room, a mere punch in the air and a look of jubilation across the room at Davey was all that was required to signal that Sunderland were promoted, we were back where we belong. Geeeeeeerrrrrrriiiiiiinnnnnn! Yes.

Only days until I could sample my first taste of live action and now to be enjoyed in the comfort zone of automatic promotion, thanks to Crystal Palace… now there's something I don't say often.

Monday 30th April 2007

I arrive at work with a wry smile, smugly written all over my mug.

"Here he is, we didn't expect you in today, never mind on time," came the startled greeting from my work colleagues.

"Nothing to celebrate yet boys, the Championship's not in the bag until next week," I responded coolly, although inside my heart was belting with pride, throbbing up to my throat, itching to explode into a fit of celebration. Meanwhile, my head was in bits, feeling like I'd been hit by a train, with the grim reaper hanging around to pour lemon juice in my wounds. In truth, the Championship would be nice to win, but promotion was the main goal.

Now to try concentrating on work when my mind was firmly on the adventures in Luton next week and the prospect of Liverpool, Manchester United and the Scumbags to play next season. It would be fair to say that not much work was produced today, something the lads would say about me all year round anyway, to be fair.

MAY

Wednesday 2nd May 2007

I am currently flying over the Alps, with a deep blue evening sky separating my near empty Boeing 737 from the long sugar glazed mountain tips. I remember whinging on about flying to Afghanistan, implementing the fact that I was accustomed to watching these fabulous examples of European terrain flash by on chartered holiday flights. Well my friends, normality is resumed, absent is the sand of Syrian sand dunes, replaced with glistening Western cities, settling in for the night. Furthermore it's ace. Out yonder is the sun setting on the horizon like a layered bar shot of alcohol. I imagine Blue Bols at the bottom, a touch of Cypriot Zyvania, mixed with Orange Bacardi Breezer, depicting Earth's warmest star, followed by more Blue Bols to cap off the night sky. It's magic, perhaps not to drink, but to stare at. And yes I've been on the plonk too.

It has been nine months since I last set foot on North East soil, Christ; you could have had a bairn in that period, never mind the simple feat of promotion to the Premiership. And it's an obvious nine months since I last saw close family and friends. It will be strange, like nothing has ever changed, people with the same gripes, asking me on first sight – "When do you go back to Cyprus?" Cheers mate.

I was strangely saddened to leave my adopted home in the Med. As queer as it may seem, I've grown institutionalised to watching Sunderland via Soccer Saturday, through the hazy mists of an inferno barbecue. I feel a sense of loyalty to my front TV and sitting room, they have served me proud, we've bonded well, all contributing to witnessing the good times roll in far, far away on Wearside. I'm not used to the climate of rip-off Britain, its gang warfare, muggings and asylum seekers.

Once again in my journals, I digress. Billy Vodka and his mates are on board this flight, as is Vicky Wine and I've shared plenty of conversations with them. I don't think I can even write properly at the minute, as turbulence kicks in. I once would be concerned about my plane rattling between varying altitudes, but after the Afghan roller coaster ride, I don't give a shit anymore. Maybe they should take people afraid of flying to the desert, that would sort them out. I am a tad concerned about the metal wing flapping away though. It will all be worth it though to see the sights of my parents' faces. This will extinguish any fears and traumas of flying home. I believe in fate, Quinn and Keane.

The trouble is our lass never experienced any turbulence, or flapping of the aircraft wings… time to lay off the booze, methinks.

Thursday 3rd May 2007 am

We arrive early doors Thursday morning at the Tyne and Wear Airport. As usual the old man is late, however, the passing figure of Stan Varga graces my presence. Is this an attempt from the club to praise my loyalty in travelling so far to see my team? Has my family secretly set up a Surprise, Surprise style welcome? The end result is neither, as Varga flashes by, spouting over his mobile in what I presume is street Slovakian spiel.

My Dad arrives soon after, pleased to see us and it's not long before we're settled back in Sunderland, tired and weary, but happy to be home. We are treated to homemade spaghetti bolognese and even though it's the early hours, the meal flies off my fork and down my throat, quicker than a whippet with a rocket up its arse. I'm handed numerous copies of Sunderland paraphernalia in a scene reminiscent from nine months previous. I'm off to bed, to rest my mind in preparation for the shenanigans of the day ahead and no doubt copious amounts of drink.

Thursday 3rd May 2007 pm

Our lass and I exchange words about how she's off to see her mates, leaving me in the lurch. We had agreed beforehand to do our own thing, as last time it was like panic stations trying to cram in visiting family and friends. Do people realise they can actually visit us; there is no monopoly on us having to trek around to see them? Anyhow, this had been a bonus, but I'd thought I'd play on it somewhat, to earn brownie points, when I needed them.

Imagine the scene…

Our Lass: "What you want to go out with yer mates on the only Friday night we're in the UK?"

Me: "Well you did go out the other day (Thursday) with your friends, so it's only fair…"

OL: "Well I suppose…"

And you understand where I'm coming from. Besides, doing our own thing gave me ample opportunity to ramble around my hometown, visiting old haunts (pubs) and in particular popping down the ground to pay my respects to the greatest football club in the world (present or not) and more importantly nip to the Sunderland supporters' shop once more, to lustfully gain more memorabilia from this bizarre season of ours. This time the total bill soared to just under £75 in away matchday programmes, all worthwhile, all examples of our remarkable rise. The sneaking around was all creditable, with the end results ambling through past previews of Sunderland from diverse perspectives ranging from Barnsley to Bury, Preston to Norwich. The self-salivating exercise was soon brought to an abrupt end, as my dad shouted through to the garage the imminent arrival of our lass, fresh from her shopping escapade in Eldon Square, or wherever.

From her fleeting meet and greet with me her hubby, she was soon off to Sunderland to complete her shop, whilst I sought refuge in local alcohol amenities such as The Grange, Mill View Social club (in which I played dominoes of all things) The 'old' Flying Boat, followed by a curry at The Shagorika. It was here the night's proceedings caught up with Al, my brother-in-law and me, finally succumbing to high levels of booze abuse and binge drinking, by entering into a cutlery fight, in the middle of the Indian restaurant.

With a fingernail missing later (a result of my opponent's fork sliding down to the root between skin and nail) and Al clocked over the head with my spoon, we were soon shown the door, minutes after completing a chicken tikka madras, complimented by tarka dal. I then decided to take the fun fight a stage further by pretending to hold a fork to Al's throat outside on the Seaburn promenade, only for one of the other law abiding punters to rush out to hand me my coat, which I'd forgotten. His expression was one of despair, leaving us instantly to carry on with events. We made our way around the corner to see our lass and her mate, thus making holy shows of ourselves once more.

Why is it that I'm always too drunk to enjoy my Indian meal in comfort?

On my return home, I was promptly told of my teenage behaviour, with me mam asking "Wasn't it time I bloody grew up?" – a question she'd been asking for years, with me failing to answer correctly. Time for bed.

Friday 4th May 2007

My head is surprisingly fine. My stomach needs more time, but my finger is in agony, on the verge of turning brown already. No sympathy is offered from any quarter, as my mobile vibrates to the piss takings of Al and the topic of my poorly digit. Dickhead.

Still it's the weekend and the beginning of the promotion party. Open the bars…

Saturday 5th May 2007

It's the day before the final culmination of Operation Cuckoo, the final push over the top. The zenith of all the prior planning, the undercover sorties, the spying reconnaissance missions, finally leading to this combative finale, in which four of us go marching into the unknown, this time ready for a laugh and giggle.

I'm high on energy all day, as I'm left by myself once more, with our lass trying to save the troubled Joplings store single handed.

My cravings for live football cannot wait any longer and so I invite my old man to come and watch the under 18s team in action against Manchester City in the regional final of the national competition.

I enter my spiritual home of the SOL, through the clinks of the turnstiles, taking in the atmosphere. Even with the ground empty, the entire place possesses a unique quality in taking your breath away. The ground still has that old wow factor.

Even though I was only there to sit inside tapping into the awe of the arena, like some football-craving junkie, I found myself becoming involved with disputes with the referee, akin to the usual gripes of a first team game. Only this time, there were around 500 people in attendance, listening to my moans echo off the empty red seats. Still, it was a release of pent up frustration. Out came Kandahar worries, the tension of Luton tickets, all in one amalgamated voice.

A family meal is enjoyed on the evening, leading to the consumption of several bottles of wine. One eye is kept on the alcohol meter; an early rise at the crack of sparrows is required in the morning, to arrive in earnest for the silly 1pm kick off. Why do the powers that be insist on spoiling everyone's fun? Why can't all games kick off at the standard 3pm regulation? The pubs won't open until midday being a Sunday – the day of the Sabbath. I'll need a buoyant beverage or two, for me to reach my optimum performance levels to spur the lads to victory. With no alcohol allowed on football coaches anymore, I've devised a cunning plan, to go with the undercover theme of Operation Cuckoo.

I've already acquired a small crate of miniature vodkas, back in Cyprus. The plan is simple. In order for me to smuggle by illicit booze on board the bus, I will simply absorb my collection of Russian firewater into a pack of sandwiches, dubbed Vodka Sandwiches of course. The Luton tour operators will think "Canny lad, bless him, his mam's made him some bait for the journey down," when in reality my stash will go unchecked, headed for the scrum of the backseat, to be consumed as I see fit – probably all down the hatch before we're past Durham.

The lads are impressed with my sneaky scheme. I argue the point of why on earth I should resort to such lengths to enjoy a social drink, on such a celebratory occasion? Imagine the future years of football, when the country has transformed into a police state, or slumbered into civil war. In the first instance the military regime would not tolerate any kind of amusing behaviour, as this would be strictly against the law. Football fans would be escorted to games, organised solely by government officials for their own entertainment of observing supporters courted in like scum, adding to their own personal power trip hard on. The second example of a civil war, caused by rival fractions of creed around the country, would not foresee the carrying of adult pop between various states and inter party borders of control. On passing through multi regions, one's bus would be ransacked by that particular region's rebel army, leading to many a death over one's four pack of cans. The forecast is not good either way.

As my pub craic entwines into putting the world to rights, I receive a text message from Nick, one of our party of four nomadic travellers.

"Mate I cant make it 2morro summit has cum up. Sorry marra I'll xplain lata, I will still pay 4 me ticket tho. Soz mate."

Bastards! I don't believe it. I hit the roof, after all the running around, organising these precious golden tickets, that even Willy fucking Wonka wouldn't have obtained, only to be sniffed at in the final hour, well I was miffed to say the least. It must be something important to pass on this opportunity. Even though he had done the decent, noble gesture of still offering to pay for the ticket and presumably the travel, I still did not want the ticket merely to go to waste. This was Sunderland's finest match in years to be a part of, I considered shouting at the bar that there was a free match ticket going, but changed my mind after fears of becoming mobbed.

One of my mates will have it, I pondered, swiftly engaging in a fleet of text messages. To my surprise and shock, everyone had an excuse, or an event in the way. My mate Leigh, who I'd shared the delights of Cardiff with back in 2005, was pissed to hear of my freebie on offer, especially as he had travelled up from his Southern dwellings, only to be a godparent at a christening. Some of the things he cursed via mobile would soon see him barred from church for life, if spoken out loud. Operation Cuckoo was a man down, but we'd soldier on, ready to face tomorrow's proceedings, already adapting to overcome the hurdles that would be thrust in our way. Onwards and upwards, I say.

We return home from the local public house, mildly inebriated, but still in control of our bearings, which was more than important, as our lass prepared a humble French loaf, exasperating her culinary skills to a new found height, to provide Operation Cuckoo with supplies of the now famous Vodka Sandwiches.

Vodka Sandwiches – The Secret Recipe

Ingredients

1 x Stottie cake (or if left to the last drunken minute – a French loaf)
12 x Mini bottles of vodka

1 x Roll of cling film
1 x Glass of red wine (preferably a Merlot grape)
Butter (optional)

The method

1) Firstly pour yourself a glass of Red wine, as this dish is best prepared in a tipsy mood.

2) Next hold your choice of bread and hollow out the insides, making plenty of room to insert one's miniature bottles of spirit.

3) Find the slab of vodka and break down the pallet.

4) Wrap the individual consignments of vodka in a wrap of cling film. This will keep the package of alcohol intact, during any rocky moments on one's journey as well as disguising the distinctive clinking sound of rattling vodka bottles.

5) Place the outer slice of crust seared away for the initial opening of the loaf back into its original position, to avoid any detection if interrogated or searched on arrival.

6) As stated the usage of butter is optional. If the user deems the sandwiches to be of use after the primary task of concealing one's drink has been achieved, then the application of butter/margarine can be inveigled into the inner core of one's loaf.

7) With the scooped out bread, apply the chef's choice of jam/marmite/other sandwich spreads and finish off with the half drunk red wine, thus creating two meals with one loaf, resulting in a basic beer supper.

8) Finally, place the vodka sandwiches in tin foil, to further harness any detection from scrutinising bus company officials and insert into a plastic carrier bag, preferably of the cheap and nasty supermarkets, once again off putting for the would be little Hitler of the highways.

Serving Suggestion

After the prolific high quality loopy juice is dispersed from its baked package, proceed to serve with a fizzy pop of your choice, most notably Diet Coke or Iron Bru.

Alternative Ingredients

This recipe also works well when the vodka is replaced with whiskey, brandy, gin or rum and/or all four top shelf components.

And with that, I'm off to bed, to rest my knackered soul, in preparation for the big day and the onset of Operation Cuckoo.

Sunday 6th May 2007

I've woke up early all week, still based on Cyprus time (two hours ahead of GMT) and so the problem of tossing and turning in bed while the rest of the household is fast asleep, has been a burden plaguing my wits with exhaustion all week. This morning though, the wide awake syndrome is a welcome relief, as my mobile alarm clock is as dodgy as Del Boy's market stall and I need to be up and ready before the early birds have caught their worm.

Today is the day I have spent over twenty months agonising over, climbing the walls of a make believe guard, restricting my movement, hoisting a cordon around any footballing arena in which Sunderland are on display. Not since Chelsea away at Stamford Bridge in September 2005 have I seen my red and white heroes at first hand and I plan to make up for lost time.

Obviously with my Cypriot insomnia, I am the first one awake, closely followed by our lass, who is on standby to travel with us down to Luton, therefore utilising the spare ticket situation enforced upon us from last night. She still possesses a passing interest in football and Sunderland as her main club. She was once a season ticket holder at Roker Park, but has now evolved a love hate relationship with the game; thanks mainly to my own dominating stance on eat, sleep and drink football. She is up for the match, but not for the long journey down to Bedfordshire.

Asleep downstairs coincidentally is my sister (Birthday Girl) who came down from Edinburgh for the weekend. We joked that she should attend her first game, especially as she was the star attraction on the half time scoreboard. How peculiar it would be if the spoof reason on which we were basing our white lies on would now in fact be a true event, after all, despite the age difference of four years. However, it was the laborious journey down south that would be the un-doing of that scenario. Birthday Girl was staying put.

In the end we would have to travel down to Sunderland's most poignant match in recent times one fan light, hoping to distribute the ailing ticket to some desperate soul in and around Kenilworth Road.

Through the ordeal of citing potential suspects to take up this amazing free offer, the old man and I forgot the time, meaning we were nearing the pick up time at the SOL and we were still back in the house. Drastic measures meant that our lass was succumbed into giving us a lift down to the ground in her pyjamas.

Ged was already waiting, having been left to his own devices many a time in the past, commenting that I live in my own version of GMT. Today though he wasn't bothered, as I told him the news of the vodka sandwiches, the lads in charge let us on board. I made sure I was near the front of the queue to get on in order to claim the prized asset of the back row of seats. This particular vicinity of the coach would allow us to revel in the shrouded air of secrecy, a vital element to carry out our covert operation involving our bag of booze. The added bonus of the bus bog situated directly in front of me would enable us to drink in peace, whilst enjoying only a small walk to relieve our bladders.

The fact that we were not searched (which in fact was the only ounce of common sense witnessed all day) was also in tune with our good fortunes thus far. As the old man embarked on a journey into the land of nod, a position he held for most of the way down and back, Ged and I tucked into our supply of goodies, having just passed Seaham. I have to say that even though these were the first vodka sarnies I had tasted, they were sublime, something I may share with Gordon Ramsay the next time we meet. And yes we ate the bread too.

We were going great guns, bombing down the motorway. At this rate, we'd be there before any of the pubs were open. We wouldn't be the first Mackems in town though. Al would make sure of this. If I thought the consumption of alcohol was a major part of my match day routine, then just consider his eccentric case. Not content with the idea of merely smuggling spirits on board the away coaches, he and one other booked a flight to London Stansted, via Sunderland's old foes easyJet. The daft bugger would then arrive in Essex at 8am, catching a train into London and up to the confines of Luton. All this to appease his inner addictions to match day drinking, providing him with the perfect backdrop of routine train services, where he could consume his checked in flight bags full of a consortium of lager and top shelf patter. Now that is definite loyalty to the beer. Once again it displays just how far Sunderland fans will go to support their team and have a good time. Imagine if the club ever reached the dizzy heights that the likes of Liverpool have enjoyed in the past few seasons, in reaching two European Cup Finals. I'm pretty sure all flights out of England would be brimming to capacity, with the red and white alliance on board. It is an overwhelming and scary thought. For now though my thoughts return to the basic issue of the Lads getting hold of the Championship trophy.

On that subject I read in my Football Echo that the old lady on top of one of the most famous trophies in the world (having once been the original crown of English football) will not be present at either Luton or Preston, where Birmingham are in town today. Apparently, the league does not present the end of season award at away grounds, due to health and safety. What a load of crap. Health and safety? Fuck me, if things continue in this vain, no one will be able to take a dump in their own toilet due to health and safety. I can foresee government officials in our future Police state, enforcing homeowners into quarantine once an example of faeces has been passed. Fans pay good money to see their team achieve success and when that opportunity comes along, some prick in a suit who receives more in salary than a culmination of an entire row of season tickets, has taken it from under everyone's noses. It's complete bollocks; there is no other word in the English vocabulary that best sums it up.

This subject only fuels our back seat debate on the coach, as we polish off more of our Russian bottled friend.

Our driver instructs us that he needs a break and we're off to the next services en route. Time for a paper, a bit craic and more vodka. The old man, now awaken from his slumber, has placed himself on high paranoia alert, instructing us to be careful when consuming our forbidden goods, even forming a careful evaluation of how to dispose of any evidence in the nearby bins. I respond with a care-free attitude, supplied by the aforementioned tipple, adding that neither the FBI or CIA were the slightest bit interested in the bombardment of our livers and so it wasn't a criminal matter of life or death in these circumstances. However, we knew the rules and if any signs of evidence were left on the bus as we headed anywhere near the jurisdiction of the Bedfordshire constabulary, then we would be told to turn around and head back North, ruining everyone's day out. We knew from experience this may be the case and so all empties were discarded, with the remaining few full bottles closely enveloped in our clothing.

As far as we were concerned this was to be the last stoppage before heading towards Kenilworth Road. Wrong. On arrival at the outskirts of the county, we were once again informed of another service station break. As we were still well in advance of any pub opening times, the passengers were happy to stop off for five to ten minutes, refresh and set back on our way. The driver told us it would be a longer envisaged break of up to twenty minutes, namely because the local constabulary required all the coaches to enter Luton town centre in one complete convoy. At this stage, I had already smelt a tinge of bullshit, which might affect our onward journey.

On return from the mind blowing extortionately priced facilities (surely something has to be done about this rip off Britain culture), we were greeted with the news that we were facing further delays of over forty five minutes, as the coppers kept us prisoner, like hostages, in another throwback to 1970s discipline. I tried to muster the lads into a theme tune of The Sweeney but no one was in the mood.

Now I can understand the significance of a roadblock mentality from the police in high security football matches, in cases such as local derbies, notorious rival hooligan elements and the past historical aspect of a clash of enemies. Are Luton Town, already relegated, versus Sunderland, already promoted, with only a select few fans with enough loyalty points, likely to cause bother? I admit there will be a fair few thousand fans situated in the wrong areas of the ground, but not in the massive numbers the police have prepared for. You would think an entire battalion of thugs were on their way to wreak havoc and pillage the local community. No other sport excretes such prejudice as football. It is a shocking state of affairs. We are akin to second-class citizens as soon as we pull on a replica shirt or purchase an over priced ticket. Do the authorities that be not understand that a hostile situation is far more likely to occur by dick-dancing normal mellow people around, herding them like pigs, undermining their welfare, with fewer rights than your average dole-walling dickhead. It's a fact that football fans have fewer privileges as a human being than stray dogs that walk the streets. Surely something should be done about these social atrocities. If we were dolphins, bears or any other endangered wildlife, the do-gooders would be out protesting in front of Westminster. The fact this behaviour is overlooked could mean the demise of football, endangering the nation's most loved sport, not to mention a lucrative business for various enterprises all over the country. For now though, I will stand down from my high horse, retreat from my public speaking pillar, as I've transport to organise, to remedy the baffling situation on our hands.

Ged and I swiftly move to the petrol station adjacent to the detained buses. We obtain a taxi telephone number and order a dodgy one man band bastard of a taxi company.

"I'll be there in five… make it ten minutes…" twisted the voice at the other end.

Then ten minutes later…

"I'll be there in five, promise, mate," lied the bastard.

I was about to ask him if he was undercover for the local police when salvation arrived in the form of two Sunderland fans, adorned in the religious colours of red and white, filling their car with diesel.

By now there was a growing crowd of disgruntled fans, deciding on making their own journey into Luton, tired of the heavy-handed crowd control. The lad pouring the fuel interacted first…

"What's going on here mate?" came the opening interaction, with him inquiring into the large numbers of people dotted around the forecourt.

This was our chance to impose on his curiosity, we saw there were three spare seats in the back of his Jaguar and decided to take advantage of the situation.

"The coppers are keeping us here until quarter to one, to stop any bother," we yelled, much to the bemusement of our new found friend.

"That's ridiculous! So you're waiting here 'til then?" asked the Jag man.

"We were wondering if we could be cheeky and pinch a lift off you to the ground?"

The deal was done. We informed our coach driver of our plan and scurried across to our waiting ride. Now this was the way to arrive at a potential title-clinching match. It was fortunate our numbers were down to three, or we would have still been waiting for that taxi, which incidentally never rang back, dodgy geezer. It turned out our two new mates were in fact from the Midlands area and were second-generation exiled fans. They both had season tickets and attended every away game – fair play to them.

If only their directions into Luton were as positive as their loyalty to the club.

"We're useless at finding our way, don't suppose you boys know which turn off for the ground?" laughed the co-driver.

We joked back, but not for long when it transpired they were serious. In the end we opted for Luton South, which was a 50-50 gamble. We lost. Not to worry though; Luton can't be that big, someone will know the way. Four people later and we found our man, someone actually English, who pointed the way through the town centre and beyond.

After circling the area like one of the airliners overhead on approach to Luton Airport, we finally struck gold, identifying the ramshackle eyesore of a ground we all presumed was the home of Bognor Regis Town, or someone similar, as Kenilworth Road. Time was now ticking away, as we u-turned back into the shopping arcade, landing a direct hit into the heart of a standstill traffic jam. The driver told us to jump out here and he would sort parking out in a minute. We didn't need telling twice, escaping the perilous bumper to bumper scrum of cars, now on foot in search of public houses and more importantly our entrance into this football maze.

Not only was it a hellhole of a place to find oneself (and they say the North is grim – I'll take it any day) we just could not locate any boozers, nor our way around the ground. We decided to cancel the search of alcohol nourishment and concentrated on giving away our spare ticket, without looking like touts in front of the massed ranks of the local constabulary. We followed various Sunderland fans en route, leading us to the away turnstiles, where surely someone must need a ticket. At this stage of events, our original mode of transport arrived under stringent police escort. Needless to say the lads on the bus were pissing themselves in laughter, with us only arriving at the ground a few minutes before them. We should have stayed put on the bus, saving us the bother of locating the tin pot shed of a ground.

One minute stewards were shoving us in one direction, then ordering us in the other, as we asked where our entry points were in the ground. Obviously we had special tickets, as no one seemed to know where we were. Finally we had to cut between alleyways, back through the red and white glitz of the official Sunderland end, cut through more redundant alley ways, mingle past the home end massive, which brings us onto our neutral location of the Family Stand area. On our voyage back on ourselves (Kenilworth Road is only accessible through either ends of the ground, with one stand backing onto a railway line) we bumped into a group of lads, after one more ticket for their entourage. The lad's look of sheer delight when I handed over our spare ticket was priceless. Apparently, Luton Town fans were selling the same match tickets for over one hundred pounds. Mine was going for free; although the lad gave us a few quid "for drinks" which I feel displays the camaraderie between like-minded Mackems.

With the ticket now in the safe hands of a keen fan, we promptly strode around this concrete jungle to take up our seats. Considering both sides' fates had already been sorted, the atmosphere in and around the ground was borderline on tense. We overheard conversations from home fans, stating they would rather give tickets to Sunderland fans than the expected protesters, clearly unhappy at their club's freefall into the lower division. There were also comments that suggested otherwise. Messages had been broadcast all week over the internet, that any travelling Mackem, would be knifed if found in the home end. At least we were in the Family Stand then.

I found it quite apt that the Hatters' ground had the luxury of the Eric Morecambe Suite to fall back on. Quite apt in the sense that without showing too much disrespect, this really was a joke of a ground. After climbing up scaffold like staircases, we headed down darkened walkways. On arrival at our seats, we found that someone had the indecency to erect one of the floodlights directly in front of our view of the Sunderland goal. No wonder these tickets were £17 each. I couldn't knock the scene in front of the home goal, as we were afforded a direct passage to the nets.

This was it. Finally I'd entered a football ground, where my team were playing. This was the climax of all my needless anxiety, worrying over flights, arguments with our lass and endless months of hope, aspiring to be present at a game of football. All the smarting of late night defeats witnessed in Afghanistan was forgotten. All the frantic Saturday afternoons in front of the TV all banished from my short-term memory, still held on reserve, in order to appreciate this pinnacle of a moment in future years.

As you can imagine the terrace chants were all Sunderland, as echoes of Keano, Niall Quinn's Discopants and their ilk reverberated off the small interior of Kenilworth Road. And then the moment, I'd waited for… the entrance of the red and white cloth, with Sunderland chants greeting the Lads onto the pitch. Precious, precious moments indeed, as a shiver arches down my spine, all bodily hairs stood to attention, ready for the action ahead.

We all agreed beforehand that if Sunderland scored, we would hesitate first to gauge the reaction from the home sections. I'd already heard more rumblings of discontent when I made the unwelcome trek to the toilets. Inside the underground mine-like pissers, mutterings about people being threatened were heard. I kept me head down, clearly dressed in independent clothing, distanced from either club, only subject to abuse if I opened my gob, releasing my North East dialect into the air.

After two minutes, our ploy to hesitate before celebrating was deemed to be the best decision so far in this deployment of Operation Cuckoo. Anthony Stokes took full advantage of the piss poor shambles that was the home defence, by slotting away a side foot strike into the net. I sat still, stuck to the seat, my dad likewise, with Ged ignoring orders, punching the air with a gasp of "Yeeessss" under his breath. The lad who had our spare ticket must have tuned into the unwary tension of the place, settling for a wry smile to himself and a nod in our direction. As we contained ourselves, half the ground erupted around us. None more so than in the Main Stand to our right, over our shoulders. Tens of rows of travelling Mackems celebrated in style. To our front, in the supposed no go home end, pockets of fans celebrated likewise, causing scuffles, which in turn developed into arguments and full scale fights. I looked to the heavens in disbelief.

Who the hell were these Luton twats, intent on ruining our big day? Not happy at selling inflated price tickets to Sunderland fans in the first place, they now wanted a dig at them for daring to pay over the odds to see their side, in such a shit hole dump anyway. Tossers.

A few were ejected, although it turned out these were mainly Luton fans fighting amongst themselves, arguing the point of whether the Mackems were welcome or not. I've never seen anything like it. I knew we were relatively safe situated in our family seats, however it only took a wrong word or two and it would have all kicked off here too. And so the situation was hardly tamed by the curling belter from Daryl Murphy, which I caught the end of, now too busy watching the public disorder to my right. Once more, the same said areas rejoiced in the wonder strike, once more sparking disturbances, all over the ground.

One father quietly crept out of the Luton home end, holding his son's hand, both adorned in Sunderland attire. Clearly these scenes proved too much for him, quite rightly seeing his lad's safety as the paramount of importance. Just a shame the idiots had ruined their day out.

Eventually calm was restored and everyone settled down (bar the official Sunderland supporters behind our goal and the mass of fans alienated in the Luton Main Stand) to watch the Lads completely dominate the game. Carlos Edwards was booed every time he had the ball, although this practice soon died away, as Town fans lost whatever heart they had left, by the sight of Sunderland's men against Luton's boys. I'd been through all of this before myself watching the red and whites, so I understood how they felt, making this all the more sweeter for myself, enjoying my day, even if watched emotionally from afar. I felt like Keano, coolness on the outside, chuffed to bits inside. It was Sunderland themselves who calmed the entire stadium down, turning this competitive fixture into a training kick about.

Half time arrived, meaning the chance to see my sister's name in lights for a fake birthday and her name over the stadium sound system. To be honest this was forgotten about at first, after the mixture of emotions witnessed in the first half. We were given a laugh though, when the loudspeaker crackled her name and age, stating that she was an avid Luton fan. This awoke our attentions from the match, as we hastily moved around the view of the pylon, to see the scoreboard repeat the facts given by the PA announcer. We were in fits of laughter, thinking if only she could see this now. I tried to take a photo, but sod's law dictated that the scoreboard would instantly transform into the next well-wisher's message the moment I aimed my camera at the big screen. This brought light relief, shifting the focus from the serious business of avoiding a kicking, to realising what today was all about – enjoying the moment, the day, the unexpected early promotion.

The second half began in the same vain as the previous forty-five minutes, a stroll for Sunderland, the home side having already conceded defeat. During the break, we knew that it remained level at Deepdale between Preston and Birmingham, still just enough for Brum to win the title. This did not deter the Lads, Daryl Murphy once again finding the net, leaving the home fans dejected. The atmosphere was now relaxed, the odd home fan making their way to the exits already. Ross Wallace then fired a fourth, before the real celebrations began away in the Main Stand. News filtered through that Preston had taken the lead, if it remained as it was Sunderland would be champions, yet again.

I took the sublime information in a calm manner, something I have never encountered at a football match before. The vodka had long worn off, in search of the ground, this a particularly helpful factor in my muted glory. The noise was amplifying at a gradual rate, Nyron Nosworthy being the main topic of tune. I'd never heard the Amy Winehouse hit Rehab before today (the 1991 time warp zone in Cyprus was the probable reason) but the terrace version soon caught hold of my imagination. The tune circled in the territory for what seemed an eternity, harping back to the Roker Park Main Stand crazy corner era of Denis Smith's Red and White Army chants, bouncing off the eardrums for hours on end, eventually reaching a hardcore rave speed, ending in chaos and mock riots.

David Connolly rounded off the scoring with Sunderland's fifth, changing the choice of anthems from Winehouse to Kay C and the Sunshine Band. What a performance for me to enjoy. A mass exodus of white jerseys signalled the end of the road of persistence for the home support, leaving us to enjoy the remnants of the match in full comfort of spare seats, to rest our cramped bodies. The sparsely filled ground meant the echoing of the Sunderland choir was magnified, yet still we remained professional in the name of Operation Cuckoo. Now was not the time to lose our cool, be kicked out of the ground and miss the mass celebrations.

A bolt of lightning this time fizzed up my spine, as the final score was confirmed from Lancashire, with a 1-0 home win. That was it, we had the title in our midst, maybe I'd hang around for the open top bus homecoming.

This news was met with police horses, Alsatian dogs, truncheons, CS gas canisters, armoured cars, Dick Jones, OCP and Robocop. The loudspeaker confirmed that any Sunderland fan daring to run on the pitch for a moment of innocent fun with their heroes would be shot by automatic machine gun and sold to the local kebab house for the natives to munch on. Honestly, you'd have thought that every travelling fan had just been told their life savings had been spent by the government to fund a Geordie council giro bill the way the mood changed, once it looked like the title was on the cards. Is the participation of fun deemed legal anymore in England?

The three shots of the referee's whistle signified our anti-climatic return to the top flight, but the manner in which the Championship was regained (this time hopefully the last) could only be described as truly awesome. To be fair the Luton fans around us held their hands up and stated that the gulf between the two sides was immense, something one could add about the comparison between the Premiership and its poorer brother. Let's not go there just yet, and immerse ourselves instead in basking in grandeur as Carlos Edwards swings off the crossbar, Nyron dons a trilby hat and the whole team practise the European style collective one hundred metre sprint down towards the red and white followers. No doubt this is a merely an audition for next season when Europe is reached.

The Family Stand around us moped off into the twilight of the Sunday afternoon, though some Luton followers stayed to show their respects to the Champions from the North East. I took immediate advantage, clambering down seats, to perch on the front row. Other closet Mackems did likewise, all leaning over the barriers, applauding, cheering, fists aloft with satisfaction. I was meanwhile trying to clap the team, now waltzing up to our end, whilst simultaneously taking flamboyant arty photos, through my ancient model of a digital camera. I must have looked like a one-man band, trying to play all his instruments at once, while in reality, not achieving anything. I concentrated on the photos, leaving the roars of approval to my budding Operation Cuckoo-ites.

The away end sang on and on and on some more, serenading Bedfordshire to their hearts' delight. We made our way to the exit, not wanting to miss out on the atmosphere, still requiring a safe passage through the loitering home support. The hostilities had ended, even though chants of "Your going to Hartlepool, we're going to Liverpool" from the opposite end, tested the water. We were forbidden from re-tracing our steps around to the away end, as a barrier of fluorescent jackets scowled at anyone looking to head towards the Sunderland delegation. We didn't even bother to question the decision and state we were actually Sunderland fans ourselves, as they would have probably arrested us for attempting to deceive Luton Town Football Club or words to that effect. We promptly marched down to the town centre. We were now in search of off licences for alcoholic refreshment, in order to savour our sweet victory in the name of several cans of lager, of whatever denomination, it did not matter.

After having our eyes ripped out over the biggest rip off since Peter Reid paid millions for the walking money laundry that was Tore Andre Flo, we reluctantly handed over extortionate amounts of money for our beer. We sneaked past the battle line of coppers, our stowage carefully hidden under my jacket, to jump on board the promotion express, non-stop all the way back to the North East. Whilst sitting, swapping Kenilworth war stories with the lads in our back seat dwellings, the silhouette of Al waded past the coach window. He was all set to climb up the stairs of his rail replacement bus, stricken parallel to us, when a simple knock and wave with a can in my hand, caught his eye. We teased the rest of the train lads with our stash, gently pulling away to hit the motorway home. How I bet he wishes he were on board now, on cruise control back up the M1, arriving back home in plenty of time to hit the social club for bingo and then on to the town, to revel in the pandemonium. Back to London for you my lad.

The bus fell strangely quiet, perhaps the day's events taking its toll on the heartstrings. I drift in and out of visionary daydreams, eventually resting my lids for forty winks…

It's then that the signs for the motorway services perk me up, awakening me from my idle daydream and I take another swig from my now lukewarm can.

A quick stretch of the legs in reality, then back on board to enhance my dreams of the day into angelic fantasies, my eyes closed, mellowing in the memories of a perfect day...

"Ere, Mal, Roeder's been sacked," Ged shouts down my eardrum dragging me away from my daydream and back into the halcyon daze of flat overpriced lager and a bus chugged its way back up the A1.

I next woke up with a half empty can, our coach hitting the outskirts of North Yorkshire. The anticipation grows as each mile passes, dropping the odd person off at nominated points. Finally, signs for Sunderland, the biggest city in the North East region, are spotted. The iconic features of Penshaw Monument creep over the protruding hill, a kind of unofficial beacon to announce our arrival back in the heartland of Wearside.

Everyone on board is itching to alight, ready to head for their respective locations, to bathe in the loopy juice of their choice. Personally, I shall take up the old adage of a shit, shower and a shave routine, to refresh and re-stock, take in the day's events ready to relay at first hand to the eager listeners back at The Mill View Club. Our returning legions of hardy battlers have returned from frontline sections, or so you'd imagine, judging by the raised decibels of hoarse voiced old timers, proud to see their red and white offspring carrying the good name of Sunderland to feverous, distant lands, once a job they took upon themselves, back in the day. I can liken it to a Shakespearean play, or Roman script in the social...

"And what news does one bring of the immortal victory at Kenilworth?" asks the club secretary.

"Kenneth, I bringeth topper news from afar; the Red and White Saracens have acquired control of the summit of the league. Wild dogs, savage boars and ye olde Robocop stood in our way, yet we cometh from battle scarred with pride, pissed from drink," replies the warrior.

Yet in reality it went something like...

Davey: (in a pissed voice) "Ow son, any good? It was like a fucking training match like, wannit?"

Me: (trying to get a word in edgeways) "Aye Dave, top class marra, five star, different class..."

Davey's mate Lee (in a totally pissed voice) "Wwwhhyy eeezz worked fuckin wonders, that bassstard Keane, I fuckin love im."

The crowd in the background now join in with chants of Keano and Championees as we leave the play to bow out to its audience.

And bow out to our audience we did, although I'd guess nobody was watching, too busy marking off bingo numbers to care. Yet in the gentlemen's lounge, bingo for tonight was cancelled… by order of the red and white committee, for one night only.

Everyone was up for the celebrations; you could be mistaken for thinking Sunderland had won the European Cup. It has been two years since we last won the Second Division title, though I never encountered scenes as delirious as this then. Maybe it's the renewed optimism of our new Irish backers. Whatever it is, it's brilliant to be a part of, you get the feeling that this is the sort of magic carpet ride that Saint Niall was on about back in July.

Singing songs, cheap beer, quality craic, all served on a platter in abundance. I even ended up with a Sund-Ireland scarf wrapped around my neck, perhaps as a token gesture, my version of a Sunderland Military Medal, presented with full honours.

To finish off this finest of days, only one kind of beer supper would suffice. That's right ladies and gentleman… may I present the Ruby Murray, or simply Ruby to her friends.

There is nothing more sublime than to watch the highlights of the Championship title clinching game, engrossed in the oral delights of a chicken tikka madras, surrounded by your family.

A television set - £400.

One chicken tikka madras, with extra chillies - £5.50

Sunderland winning the league and avoiding any curry stains on God's cloth – priceless!

Monday 7th April 2007

I pinch myself. Not to see if I dreamt the day before, merely to see if I'm still alive, after poisonous levels of alcohol were reached. Ouch! I'm still here, still in the land of the living, thank Keane.

How on earth do I rekindle the rest of my days, surely they will be on a downward slope after yesterday's positive debacle? Nothing can match yesterday. Or can it? We move on, standards are now higher, Quinn and Keane have raised the bar and the supporters will expect.

News breaks today that the club have politely rejected the council's offer of an open top bus parade through the city. One half of me is disappointed, the other mesmerised by the originality our new club dictates. Firstly, I would love to see the whole region celebrate our achievement, considering the Football League's refusal to acknowledge the presentation of a trophy on the final day of the season. The latter half subscribes to the sentiment of Keane, that "nothing has been achieved yet." After all, Sunderland has experienced more open top bus parades than an average day's sightseeing tour around London.

Memories of the previous day come flooding back, as our lass flicks through shots from the camera. Suddenly find pains shooting through my body. One, a relapse of woe in my brain and two, a sudden juddering of bowel movements, ready to extinguish the Tikka Madras, at full pelt. Excuse me.

Thursday 10th May 2007

On the day the current Labour Prime minister, Tony Blair, serves notice on his days in power at Downing Street. I hereby draw time on the 2006/07 season's diary entries.

We arrived back on the island of Cyprus today, although the notorious sunshine we'd come to expect was replaced with incessant drizzle, ruptured by the occasional rumble of thunder, relieved by its tag team partner, lightning. The world has gone mad. In April we saw earthquakes in Kent and now at the start of summer, this isle surrounded by Mediterranean waters is eclipsed by muggy rain, not rays of light.

We travel back at the break of dawn, back to reality, away from my homeland. One, who was unsettled at leaving his adopted home in the sun, now feels the same on his arrival. As the week passed, Southern European time transcended into GMT, meaning I was out of sorts by the time I returned.

Work was delved straight back into at the deep end, deplaning straight off our flight, a drive home and into work around 7am. This in all honestly helped enormously. Although I would have been grateful for the rest and recuperation, after a hectic week and return journey, the immersion of occupational duties meant a huge wake up call. The football season was now over. No more time to dwell on the success on the current campaign. The end of the season hinted to the fact that all experiences invoked during that timescale, should be laid to rest. Not in any sense to be forgotten, more so to be respected, to be taken with us and engaged in future scenarios.

The preliminary stages of notification to go to war. The early bouts of paranoia and anxiety about what lay ahead. The overwhelming sense of camaraderie existing in the forces today, in what can only be described as a thankless task. The feeling of emptiness on my supposed triumphant return home from conflict. The engagement of stress, as Sunderland perform heroics in a footballing sense, losing only one game in 2007, yet possessing that unique fear one has following the club that at any stage, things could go so horribly wrong. And finally, the relief and personal chuckles brought about over the high levels of worry endured in those times. Both on an Armed Forces front and as a passionate football fan. Those bouts of inner laughter at the state I took myself into, stuck rigid in the realms of concern. If I have learnt anything from this past year, then that would be to allow my fears to vanish, remain calm and not to agonise over the complexities in life. As I only know too well from my newfound desert escapades… you only have one shot at life. There are no dress rehearsals. The shame is this, it took me from Afghanistan to Temazepam to understand this notion.

Glossary

Our Lass – A Mackem wife, aka footballing widow. In this particular case, a former follower of football, since losing interest in the game, due to her husband's frantic efforts to include the sport in every aspect of life.

Ultras – Bands of European fans/hooligans closely linked to such clubs as AS Roma, Lazio, Juventus et al.

The Red and White Tractor – My homemade bar in Cyprus, in which my outside front porch/veranda has been converted to reflect any local Wearside watering hole, adorned with souvenirs from clubs ranging from Real Madrid to Accrington Stanley. Built by my mate Spit, even if I do take the glory all the time.

Arsepiss – The projection of anal faeces in the form of frontal excretement, usually the culmination of a Mutton Vindaloo, a build up of nerves and tension, or both.

Bushy Mountfield – A gentlemen's moustache of enormous hairy proportion, linked with the 1980s fashion phenomenon. Worn loyally by the Everton legend Derek Mountfield.

Prudent Hesford – A Mackem myth or Fishwives' tale? Neither. Based on Sunderland's bulky keeper, Iain Hesford and visions of a classic face brush.

Silky Agboola - Another moustache excerpt, this time focussed on Sunderland full back Reuben Agboola and his Mexican-esque gunslinger effort.

Porn Harper – A moustache that could generate visions of classic porn flicks of cheesy grandeur. This time based on Everton defender Alan Harper.

Prim and Proper Heathcote – A reflection of cultural genius in the form of a hairy lip haircut, designed to woo the ladies and scare the opposition forwards, as worn by Sunderland defender Michael Heathcote deep in the 1980s.

Mortar Cherry – One's virginal experience of being on the receiving end of random missiles fired by the Taliban, aimed in your direction. Not nice.

Crow about – A slang saying, used in the North East region, meaning nothing to shout about.

Helmand Province – A district of Southern Afghanistan notorious for its sporadic violence, situated next to the Kandahar Province.

Ricki Lakes – Rhyming slang for the shakes, a state of delusion after drinking high levels of alcohol, or experienced through high intense illnesses or fevers.

PT Flight – Physical Training section of the RAF, in which they learn how to drill us into shape through sports activities.

Samson and Delilah – My Cyprus cats, named after Sunderland's football mascots. Well that was the deal with our lass, or she wasn't having them.

Lung Butter – A build up of phlegm that only human males seem to produce, inadvertently discharged out of the body through a series of nasal and throat gestures, in which one can adopt an Arabian Scouse accent, producing a mouthful of snot (Lung Butter) to be ejected immediately.

Dip – As in the Boxing Day variety, in which groups of hardened mad buggers plough their way through Seaburn beach, past a row of fire engines gleefully hosing them down, before galloping into the gaping North Sea. It's enough to equip females with protruding nipples, whilst converting a him to a 'shim' in the form of an inverted penis, such is the ferocity of the cold.

Wobbly Eggs – A reference used for drugs in the form of Acid Tabs, a cultural element of street life in the early 90s Sunderland rave scene.

White Doves/Christmas Trees – Different types of Ecstasy pill, with supposed varying influences of effects, depending on the narcotic flavourings laced in them.

Fizzy Paracetamols – The best kind of hangover cure, as they reach one's bloodstream in an instant, whilst leaving the patient content to drink the tablets like medicine, with no need to gag on trying to down tablets when ill.

Bunny Boiler – A strange type of woman, a fruit loop. See Fatal Attraction, with Michael Douglas.

AWOL – Abbreviation. Absent Without Leave is a military term used for someone who has deserted his Regiment, Squadron, Battalion, without permission and without authorised absence. In short, they've done a runner, which under military law is one of the most serious crimes one can commit, often leading to prison.

Brummie Zulus – A collection of football hooligans attached to the Midlands football club Birmingham City.

Pancho – The small Welsh lad from Channel Four TV series – Dirty Sanchez, following a group of pranksters around Britain.

Soul Crew – A collection of football hooligans attached to Welsh club Cardiff City.

Flight Sergeant – A senior rank of non-commissioned standard in the Royal Air Force.

UN no-go buffer zone – An organised agreement over a patch of land in between the border of Cyprus and the Turkish Republic of Northern Cyprus, in which no one resides.

The Blue Monkey – A rave nightclub in Sunderland famous for miles around for the amount of alleged illegalities that took place there. Was burnt to a cinder several years back.

Zyvania – A Cypriot aperitif drink, only to be consumed by humans when they are passed the point of no return when drunk. Has a taste uncannily like petrol.

Lambtons/Samson/Maxim – All legendary lagers and bitters produced by popular Sunderland brewery Vaux, which closed several years ago due to a scandalous decision to sell up by its parent company, causing massive job losses and depriving future generations of the sheer delights of its cracking ale.

Epilogue

It is always a proud moment for any Father to see his son achieve his dream, and this is mine.

Ever since the first time I took Malcolm to watch Sunderland play at Roker Park I could sense he was going to become a fanatic just like me.

It wasn't long after his first visit to Roker Park that his other passion for writing started to develop and he was soon to start producing his own fanzine. Such was his enthusiasm that the fanzine later became a commercial venture and involved lots of photocopying of the original production, stapling them together in time to stand on Fulwell Road selling them to the fans prior to every home game.

This passion for Sunderland AFC and writing continued over the years with articles written for various other magazines and in particular A Love Supreme which led to him contributing to the publication of 24 Hour SAFC People in October 2006 and his first real penetration into the writing world, after years of background work.

When Malcolm enlisted into the RAF there were not many occasions he could travel to see the home games but he never lost his passion for the Lads, none more so than when he was posted to the war zone of Afghanistan. His Mum and I were more concerned about his safety, constantly watching the news on TV, but whenever we were able to contact him his main concern was how Sunderland were playing and how far they had progressed up the league and to continue supplying him with the Football Echo and other sources of information.

It was during this period in Afghanistan that inspired him to write this book and I, his Mum, wife Angela and all his family wish him every success.

We are all very proud of you.

James Robinson